P9-DNQ-914

WORKERS, UNIONS AND THE STATE

WORKERS, UNIONS AND THE STATE

GRAHAM WOOTTON

HD6664
W6
1967

SCHOCKEN BOOKS · NEW YORK

99671

First published in U.S.A. 1967
by Schocken Books Inc.
67 Park Avenue
New York, N.Y. 10016

Copyright © Graham Wootton 1966

Library of Congress Catalog Card Number 67–12612

Printed in Great Britain

CONTENTS

PREFACE

The boundaries of this discussion are set by the obligations of workers in their trade (or labour) unions to the community at large, as represented by the State. I begin by summoning from political philosophy (and history) the question that, like a cry caught by a rising wind, once carried across the kingdom: 'why *ought* the citizen to obey the State?' Far from being outmoded even today, that question hovers over the returning traveller as he makes his customs declaration, and haunts the young man drafted for active military service overseas. In the United States as (and where) I am writing this introduction, the draft-card burners have been acting out the great dramatic theme of modern political philosophy. Nevertheless, in the United States generally as in other favoured lands such as Britain and Canada, obedience, if neither ungrudgingly given nor ever fully articulated as deeds, can be taken for granted. There, at least, the really interesting question is not 'why *ought* the citizen to obey?' but rather, '*by what process* does he *learn* to feel obliged to obey?'

I recall, too, that traditionally the problem of political obligation has been formulated and discussed in highly artificial terms: an individual apparently enjoying few social affiliations, but for that reason suffering few conflicting loyalties, is matched against the State, almost like some friendless matador alone with an indestructible bull in an empty, silent arena somewhere remote within Space-and-Time. In the complex here-and-now, I suggest, the individual has to be conceptualized within his many social groups, each of which has some claim upon his allegiance. Thus, for various reasons, I press political obligation into service only to grant it a quick discharge from this discussion, and proceed to replace it by what we may call civic obligation. The ultimate effect of that replacement is to turn attention from *man-as-citizen : State* to *man-in-his-various-roles : State*.

From the many relationships subsumed under *man-in-his-*

various-roles : State, I select for discussion, *man-as-worker* and *man-as-unionist : State*. I take the perspective of the ordinary worker and sketch the problem of civic obligation as it touches him—the right ordering of his several loyalties so as to give precedence to the just claims of the community, spoken for by the State (or by the Government, deemed here to be the State's 'honest broker'). I make no attempt to discuss the basis of a just claim; for arguments' sake I even assume, in the illustration offered, that the particular current claim advanced by the Government *is* just. I concentrate rather upon the prior problem of bringing about the right 'orientation' of the worker, the widening of the ambit of his loyalties, so that the Government's just claims could reasonably hope to receive due consideration. How might the worker *learn* to identify and accept such claims and to act upon them? What are the conditions under which he could be expected to recognize civic obligation and to exercise civic virtue (as we may term civic obligation excellently discharged)? I try, then, to trace the civic obligation of the worker to its sociological and social-psychological roots.

This concern of mine is in part the unexpected by-product of the researches I conducted intermittently for several years into the internal government and politics of the Draughtsmen's and Allied Technicians' Association (DATA), a trade union whose members occupy a strategic position in the British engineering industry and so in the British economy. For reasons that it would be as tiresome to recount as to read, I have yet to put the results of that work into book form, although I have published some preliminary findings.[1] One reason, however, is immediately relevant. For some years I attended the regular meetings of DATA's National Executive Committee, a privilege accorded few professional students of any trade union since Beatrice Webb was given it some eighty years ago. As, month after month, I sat in my unobtrusive corner seat in the lounge of a Bloomsbury hotel and listened to the discussions of high-level union policy, I became more and more absorbed by questions that had not even occurred to me at the outset: how is the personality (or character) of the active trade unionist

[1] "Parties in Union Government . . .", *Political Studies* (Oxford), June, 1961.

formed? What are its distinguishing features? What is the source and nature of trade-union norms (or expected behaviour)? I could not resist the temptation to read in the margins of my research subject, despite the inevitable diversion from the main task in hand.

At first, such questions were academic in the sense of being intellectually exciting rather than of immediate practical application. Soon after I became aware of them, however, the British Government began to sway in the direction of an incomes (or "guidelines") policy. Mixing regularly, by then, with these intelligent technicians, informally as well as formally, in the provinces as well as in London, I marvelled that the Government (and, I can now add, all its successors) had thought of everything except the essentials—the characters of the workers and trade unionists to whom its appeal for restraint and responsibility were addressed, and the nature of the unions to which such men and women belong. Since no better qualified student seemed to be falling over himself to say that while at the same time offering a constructive alternative, I decided to make the attempt myself, setting aside for the time being the original research project. The outcome is this essay.

The general and specific preparation for it has burdened me with many debts. Reorientating myself, a decade ago, towards sociology (in order to give more depth to my understanding and teaching of politics and history), I gained the ready help of Professor John Mogey, then university lecturer in sociology at Oxford, now chairman of the department of sociology at Boston University, and, at Berkeley in 1961, of Professor S. M. Lipset, now of Harvard University. For my first ventures into the specialized field of industrial sociology, I obtained the advice, also in 1961 but at Harvard, of Professors F. J. Roethlisberger and George C. Homans. In industrial relations, on the other hand, my guides were all English: my former colleague, Mr Arthur Marsh (now Senior Research Fellow in Industrial Relations at St Edmund Hall, Oxford); my present colleague, Mr Frank Pickstock (who, between them, persuaded me to try my hand at teaching shop stewards); and above all, Professor Hugh Clegg, then Official Fellow of Nuffield College, Oxford, now Pressed Steel Professor of Industrial Relations at the new University of Warwick. I thank them all.

On a different plane, I owe a great deal to the Nuffield Foundation, who financed the early DATA research from which this essay in part derives. I thank the Foundation for its help and the saintly patience it (or someone) has shown in the face of my repeated failure to keep to the timetable for the original project. It seems permissible, now that he has returned to Fleet Street, to thank also the particular officer of the Foundation with whom I dealt—Mr John Beavan—perhaps especially for his resourcefulness in making the administrative arrangements, which were well carried out by the London School of Economics and Political Science. DATA itself deserves acknowledgement for its generosity to a complete stranger; its original agreement to give me access to records, Conferences and above all to Executive Committee meetings survived unscathed despite a subsequent change of political 'tendency' within the Committee itself.

As to the specific substance of the work, ignoring classical and quasi-classical sources. I owe much in Part I to my former teacher in social philosophy at London, Professor Morris Ginsberg, and to Professor A. H. Maslow, of Brandeis University. I also benefited from a conversation with Dr Michael Argyle, university lecturer in social psychology at Oxford. My colleague, Dr W. E. J. McCarthy, unravelled for me some of the mysteries of official British strike statistics. My main debt in Part I, however, is to the Yale 'school', which underlines my catholic tastes, my last book[2] having been written under the inspiration of Harvard. No doubt the basic idea of a conflict between individual needs and organizational requirements is not new (it goes back almost two centuries at least to St.-Simon), but Professors Wight Bakke and Chris Argyris have perhaps done more than any others (certainly for me) to translate it into contemporary industrial terms, especially in the form of organizational theory.[3] My conversations with

[2] *The Politics of Influence*, Routledge and Kegan Paul and Harvard University Press, 1963.

[3] e.g., E. Wight Bakke, *Bonds of Organization* (first pub. 1950, second ed. by Archon Press, 1966); *Organization and the Individual*, 1952 and *The Fusion Process*, 1953 (both Yale Labour and Management Centre); in Mason Haire (ed.), *Modern Organization Theory*, John Wiley, 1959, ch. 2; E. Wight Bakke and Chris Argyris, *Organizational Structure and Dynamics*, Yale Labour and Management Centre, 1954; Chris Argyris, *Personality and Organization*, Harper, 1957.

them at New Haven in 1966 came too late to affect what I had written, but I readily acknowledge a general inspiration, particularly, since I chanced upon it first, Mr Argyris's *Personality and Organization*.

Professors Hugh Clegg and Martin Lipset have put me still further in their debt by taking the trouble to combine cool criticism with warm encouragement. I am particularly grateful to both of them for their very generous assistance. My absence in the United States during 1965-66, however, and the heavy pressure there of other work, effectively precluded a real exchange of views with Mr Clegg, whereas the wheel of fortune brought me face-to-face again with Mr Lipset. Of course, neither of these scholars can be held responsible for the essay in its final form. That disclaimer applies to all those whose names have been mentioned already. Despite many borrowings, I have, I believe, put my own stamp upon the work; in bending ideas to my own shape and pattern, I cannot suppose that I have entirely avoided error.

In revising the work and in checking references at the page-proof stage, I had a free run, once again, of the Widener Library at Harvard, as well as of the libraries of Tufts University, Medford, and of Simmons College, Boston. I wish to thank the librarians and their staffs. I thank also Miss Constance Lawn for her help in proof-reading and in the preparation of the index. Defying my wife's, Mary's, request for anonymity, I want to express my gratitude to her. She accepted uncomplainingly the many absences and withdrawals of the researcher-writer, spent herself in the preparation of the typescript, and was still taking notes of errors and infelicities in the first draft as we paced the promenade deck of the *Queen Elizabeth*.

G. W.

Warborough, Oxford,
Medford and Brookline, Massachusetts,
1965-66.

'How remote an interest or a loyalty can a man compass?'

SIR GEOFFREY VICKERS, V.C.

'. . . the loyal subject as distinct from the intelligent patriot, i.e., as distinct from the man who so appreciates the good which in common with others he derives from the state—from the nation organized in the form of a self-governing community to which he belongs—as to have a passion for serving it, whether in the way of defending it from external attack, or developing it from within. . . . That active interest in the service of the state, which makes patriotism in the better sense, can hardly arise while the individual's relation to the state is that of a passive recipient of protection in the exercise of his rights of person and property. While this is the case, he will give the state no thanks for the protection which he will come to take as a matter of course, and will only be conscious of it when it descends upon him with some unusual demand for service or payment, and then he will be conscious of it by way of resentment. If he is to have a higher feeling of political duty, he must take part in the work of the state.'

T. H. GREEN

'But the national community is too large and remote to command this kind of loyalty and to make of it a continual driving force. That is why many people think that the solution of our problem lies in the development of more limited loyalties, to the local community and especially to the working group. In this latter form industrial citizenship, devolving its obligations down to the basic units of production, might supply some of the vigour that citizenship in general appears to lack.'

T. H. MARSHALL

PART I

Workers into unionists

CHAPTER ONE

ARE THE UNIONS IRRESPONSIBLE?

The boundaries of this essay are set by the obligations of workers in their trade (or labour) unions to the community at large, as represented by the State. Within those boundaries a small area enclosing a current issue has been crudely demarcated mainly as a focusing-device for the eye, but partly as a contribution to the debate about the issue itself. Now man's (and so the worker's) obligations to his fellows can hardly be reduced to a simple formula; nevertheless, the discussion will be advanced if we bring into position three interrelated concepts and use each in turn to pick out, as in the flickering beams of a searchlight, one facet or another of the whole shadowy pyramid of obligation. In the early modern (as opposed to medieval) period, it was the obligation of man-as-citizen to the State that first induced a gnawing concern and perplexity: why *ought* he to obey it? At first the very legitimacy of the State as an institution was at stake, but in time the gauntlet came to be thrown down rather at the instructions or appeals issued in its name. The broad answers, very crudely reproduced, included eventually: because he once signed, or may now be deemed to have signed, a contract, ushering in a society or government or both, i.e., because he once consented or may now be deemed to consent; because the State protects his natural rights; because obedience to the State is, on balance, useful to him; because the State enables him to achieve self-realization.

Political obligation in this sense was evidently of crucial importance in the sixteenth and seventeenth centuries. Already the issue of obedience had been posed more sharply than ever before by the rise of the new centralized States, activated by the new monarchs and the new bureaucrats, buttressed here and there by the new standing armies. Almost at the very same time (in the long perspective of history) the religious sanction for the exercise of political power began to weaken, and by the seventeenth century the more recent, more desperately specific doctrine—

> *Not all the water in the rough rude sea*
> *Can wash the balm off from an anointed head;*
> *The breath of worldly men cannot depose*
> *The deputy elected by the Lord*—

was so far discredited that one such deputy's anointed head (poor King Charles's) was severed from his body with reasonable dispatch and, in the circumstances, all possible surgical skill. Even today, however, *political obligation*, in a special form, has not lost its practical relevance: in how many of the new African States, for instance, can the obedience of the soldiers be taken for granted? From time to time that issue may be raised even in the older liberal democracies of Western Europe. Some of us have vivid memories of France in May, 1958 and especially in April, 1961, when, our car held up and searched at every major road-junction, we scanned the sky for the swinging dots that might grow into paratroopers, and tried to suppress the confused feeling that Time had gone into reverse—that once again it was May–June, 1940, when, bewildered, we watched a great State topple sideways and not so much collapse as lean over absurdly amid the rubble and the smoke. In more favoured lands, however, the whole issue has become academic in every sense, part of the discipline of politics in major universities rather than the stuff of politics in the workaday world. In such lands 'how?' has superseded 'why?' as the really absorbing question: *by what process* do men *learn* to feel political obligation, not *on what basis* is it justifiable and rationally to be expected?

There lies one reason why, even if *political obligation* did not come trailing clouds of glory from more heroic days and infinitely more able men (masters to my journeyman, at best), it would not serve the purpose in hand. Another reason is that the question has usually been framed in atomistic terms: isolated man confronts the State. That was a legitimate abstraction so long as the population was small, the number of social groups comparatively few, 'closed' to recruitment and 'exclusive' in membership. As populations began to multiply, however, huddling together in the great new cities; as many more social groups emerged, each increasingly 'open' and 'inclusive' and hence more and more overlapping in membership; and as the canals, turnpikes and above all the railways put such groups more and more in touch, the convenient fiction of isolated man ceased to be convenient. To say that is not to perpetuate the fallacy of reification, of misplaced concreteness, *i.e.*, of turning what is, in one important sense, an abstraction (a social group) into a reality of the same order as a 'concrete', flesh-and-blood person. Of course, thoughts are the thoughts of persons, dreams their dreams, acts their acts; social groups, having no bowels, do not experience that knife-edge twinge of compassion which is both man's distinction and privilege. Yet, although groups are not organisms, much less super-organisms, they are 'real' in the (of course, different) sense that membership in them does demonstrably influence the character and conduct of the members. Now that the stinging dust of post-1945 methodological controversy seems to be settling, it is possible for all who wish to see that *social group* and *individual* merely represent different systems of notation. Both systems can be properly used, as the great masters, innocent of methodology, demonstrated when they wrote the first chapters in the book of Western civilization. What characterizes our age, however, is the need to resort more than ever before to the *group* notation for the analysis of practical problems. Only when we have imaginatively placed man in his several social groups and watched him being buffeted by the cross-winds that thus blow fitfully upon him can we begin to understand the modern problem, gain some accurate notion of its dimensions and complexities.

In the modern world, accordingly, the pattern of obligation can no longer be represented by a few sweeping brush strokes: individual and (or versus) State. Social reality, and with it contingent obligation, is now better portrayed in the very young child's pencil drawing—hesitant, wavy lines that meander back and forth across the page without obvious beginning or plausible destination. In the social world we stand at the intersection of many lines. Often enough, obligations to colleagues at work cut across obligations to one's family; these in turn clash at times with the requirements of one's church or temple, sports or motor racing club, professional association. This is the sphere of *social obligation.* Obeying now this call, now that, temporarily deaf to others, each of us is hero and villain, martyr and egoist—or a fluttering, pale-faced harlequin anxiously displaying the colours of both.

Even to our blinkered vision, political obligation and social obligation evidently overlap; to some wide-eyed aerial photographer they might even be seen to coincide. Is political obligation, in the end, anything more than social obligation dressed up to kill? Is obligation to the State (owed in practice to other men) anything more than a special case of obligation to one's neighbours (in their several social groups)? Thus beckoned, I am tempted to respond but, resisting, I proceed on the assumption that these two types of obligation can be usefully distinguished. On the other hand, social obligation, while adding a cubit to the stature of political obligation as traditionally discussed, does not in itself meet my present requirements either. Just as politics, both the practical action and the university discipline, is about the public good (as well, that is to say, as about power), so, when political obligation is on stage, there will stand in the wings *some* concern for the 'general care' (Brabantio's phrase, in 'Othello', at that fateful meeting of the Duke in Council). To dispense with the concept, therefore, is to run the risk of abandoning that concern.

Thus I stand in need of a concept visualizing man in the complexities of his modern social setting but still taking account of the 'general care'. Conjuring up such a concept, I call it simply *civic obligation.* The term 'civic' seems always to have implied 'community', if narrowly defined: thus the 'civic garland' of Ancient Rome was awarded for saving the life of a fellow-*citizen* on the battlefield, the battle itself being doubtless interpreted as for the public good. But the term appears to have become clearly identified with citizenship (as distinct from *a city*, a mid-seventeenth century connection) only in the period when the young Wordsworth found it bliss merely to be alive. The French revolutionaries, however, did not rely upon the intoxication of the hour to secure obedience: they invented the *serment civique*—the civic oath of allegiance to the brave new world of 1789. A year later, Edmund Burke, denouncing the Revolution, was to coin 'Civick Education'; after 1871 one could speak of 'civic virtue', appropriately enough perhaps in an age usually taken as transitional between individualism and collectivism and in that sense marking the 're-discovery of community' after the lean years of 'atomization'. At all events, the adjective will serve well enough to indicate that, like political obligation, civic obligation pays tribute to the 'general care'. On the other hand, while not losing sight of the individual, it conceptualizes him within his group contexts, and so transcends the relationship *man-as-citizen: State* the better to focus attention upon *man-in-his-various-roles: State.*

In this discussion, however, I do not grapple with such great issues in their entirety; from the many relationships conceivable, I select for inquiry *man-as-worker* and *man-as-unionist: State.* My vantage point is not that of the union leaders: I have little interest in any such declaration of intent as that once made by the Indian National Trade Union Congress—to the effect that their loyalties go out, in descending order, to the Congress Party, to the government, to the nation and only then to their own union members.[1] I take instead the perspective of the ordinary worker and sketch the problem of civic obligation as it touches him—the right ordering of his several loyalties so as to give precedence to the just claims of the community, as advanced by the State (or the Government, construed as the State's 'honest broker'). I make no attempt to discuss the basis of a just claim; I even assume, in the illustration offered, that the particular current claim or appeal made by the Government *is* just. I focus rather upon the prior problem of bringing about the right 'orientation' of the worker, of widening the ambit of his loyalties, so that the State's just claims could hope to receive due consideration. How might the worker *learn* to identify and accept such claims and to act upon them? What are the conditions under which he could be expected to recognize civic obligation and to exercise *civic virtue* (as we may term that obligation very well discharged)? I attempt, then, to strip down the civic obligation of the worker to its sociological and social-psychological foundations.

In making this attempt I address myself in the first instance to the general reader sufficiently concerned with public affairs generally, and especially with a basic problem con-

[1] Myron Weiner, *The Politics of Scarcity*, University of Chicago Press, 1962, p. 78.

fronting industrial society, to be willing to follow a sustained argument that here and there requires fairly close attention. At the same time I hope to attract the professional reader too, including university and college students. I have good reason to think that specialists in industrial relations and trade unionism will find some sections of the work interesting, mainly perhaps the first two Parts. I have very much better reason for thinking that sociologists and some other social scientists will be interested in the argument throughout, fundamentally because I am really dealing with a special case of a wider problem familiar to them. In another sense, of course, I am appealing even more to specialists in politics and government, or public affairs in some less technical connotation.

All the same, my appeal is very far from being 'merely' intellectual: my purpose is also distinctly and immediately practical. For I hold strongly that current approaches to industrial issues, including the politico-industrial question of incomes policy or 'guidelines' for union wage-demands, merely plough the sand. Since I also think I can explain just why they plough the sand, I make so bold as to try to stimulate a public discussion to which the statesmen will listen and contribute, from which they will learn and upon which they will eventually act. That is hardly a modest objective, and the defence that someone has to break some new ground is more unbecoming still. I take my stand on the crucial importance of the issues and the urgency of the hour, when every voice is entitled to be heard, mine, belonging to a fully-paid-up member of the club, no less than anyone else's.

No silken advocate need be briefed to argue for 'urgency', which is only too apparent. What is ultimately at stake, however, transcends the immediate issues of public policy. Less than three generations ago, Émile Zola, moved by a tragic strike of miners in northern France, forecast (in his novel, *Germinal*)[2] the harvest that would be ours in this century. He was right in essentials, if not about the means of accomplishment. A black avenging army (Labour, of course, not miners alone) *did* slowly germinate in the furrows, and the germination

[2] Published 1885. Sometimes described as one of the four greatest French novels, but 'Oliver Edwards' (? Editor of *The Times*) dissents. 'Talking of Books', *The Times*, 1 April 1965.

has overturned the earth. That the overturning has not been done, in this country or the United States, by brute force has been our good fortune. But Labour has its revenge all the same, and it is subtler and sweeter far than the transient delights of a physical blow could ever have afforded: it is a revenge of transposition, of a reversal of legal bargaining strength in favourable economic circumstances. In such a situation it is understandable that some, crying havoc, should want to change the rules of what, to our great benefit, still has many of the features of a game. That is the angry man's remedy: even if it were right, the relationships of the past could not be revived to redress the ills of the present. What we (and some other advanced industrial countries) must do is to turn disadvantage to advantage by forcing ourselves to think out the problem afresh. That the problem is difficult no one denies; that it can be solved, if we really wish to solve it, is the burden of these pages.

I propose, then, to focus briefly upon that cluster of serious and apparently intractable post-war problems so closely interrelated as to appear one problem: inflation, balance-of-payments crises and a comparatively low rate of economic growth. Although the substance of this reference is British, the illustration itself has significance for the United States, where the danger of inflation has impelled the President, prompted by his Council of Economic Advisers, to ask union leaders to observe certain 'guidelines' when making wage-demands for their members. But even if the particular illustrative case had no relevance for the United States, the general analysis that opens in the following chapter would seem, if valid at all, to apply to her as well (I do not say *as much*) as to Britain. Thus American readers may wish to divest themselves of the particular instance and move kangaroo-fashion to the next chapter, where they will be able to read on immediately at a higher level of abstraction. British readers may follow suit if the specific issue eventually ceases to be one of urgent public importance.

*   *   *   *   *

'Inflation' may be taken here as that process in which the

money demand for the output of goods and services grows relatively to the output itself, thus tending to raise the general level of prices. In the form of a rise in retail price, inflation has been part of everyone's experience since the Second World War. By 1964 it had gone so far that a bundle of goods and services for which one would have paid £1 in 1946 cost no less than £1 17s. 4d. The value of money correspondingly declined, cancelling out much of the increases in wages and salaries. By the same token the community perpetrated on those with fixed incomes (as on the ex-Colonies to whom we were indebted in the form of sterling balances in London) a kind of theft—the worst kind, from the comparatively weak and defenceless. Economically, unless there are offsetting inflations abroad, the rise in our prices encourages imports of goods and impedes our export of them, thus making our balance of *trade* more unfavourable. Assuming, for illustration, no change in the *invisibles* (such as interest and profits on overseas investments; tourists' spending; Government spending overseas; receipts for shipping and insurance services), we then lose ground on our balance of *payments*, current account. Assuming, too, that our net position on capital transactions remains unchanged (involving such items as arise from buying or selling a factory in another country, or making an overseas loan), we have either to draw upon our reserves of gold and foreign currencies or increase our short-term borrowing or both. Our exports and economic growth suffer. The British pound sterling is one of the two key currencies in international trade (the other being, of course, the United States dollar), and from that very fact commercial opportunities come our way (e.g., to sell insurance services). As long as we are lurching towards bankruptcy (i.e., as our reserves begin to melt away), such opportunities will be fewer. Physical exports will be checked too because foreign buyers, judging that the pound is likely to lose its value, will hold back their orders: later they may be able to buy our goods more cheaply, receiving more pounds for their own currency, or having to hand over less of their own currency for a given quantity of pounds. Meanwhile, the Government will have taken various emergency measures, including probably a rise in Bank Rate to stem the tide of withdrawals of balances in London by foreign investors who want to get out of sterling before it loses its value. The rise in Bank Rate combined perhaps with a more general credit 'squeeze' may induce businessmen at home to postpone or even cancel decisions to invest in plant or buildings; certainly the gloomy prospect will reduce their confidence in the future. The smaller the investment, the lower our productivity and so the rate of economic growth.

No doubt that is but a crude sketch of a complicated process. But it goes some way to explaining what has been happening to us. In the ten years 1953–63 exports went up in volume at an average rate of 3.3% a year, but imports reached 4% a year. British exporters have worked wonders since the war, but less wonderfully than the circumstances demanded. World trade in manufactures (and our strong suit is in engineering products) has been increasing at a rate of about 8½% a year in the past decade, but our *share* in the export of manufactures has fallen from about 20% in 1954 to perhaps 14% in 1964. As late as 1950 we had had about a quarter of that trade. Between 1961 and 1964 our imports went up about twice as fast, in volume, as our exports. With increases in price as well, the outturn in 1964 was an import bill of £700 millions, the foundation for the balance-of-payments crisis in the autumn that became, by the end of the year, a deficit on current and capital account of the order of £750 millions. Meanwhile productivity (or output per worker) has been increasing slowly (I do not say only for the reason touched upon here). We have indeed improved on our pre-war (1913–38) rate of about 1½% per annum, but even at some 2% in the nineteen fifties and early sixties, we trailed behind every industrialized country in Europe.[3] With low productivity, our exports have been less competitive than they otherwise would have been . . . and so the story could go on.

But what, it may be objected, has this to do with the unions and where does their civic obligation come in? It is at least plausible to argue that the principal reason for these post-war difficulties has been our inflation (or rise in the general price level), and that the main source of that has been trade-

[3] See, *passim*, Angus Maddison, *Economic Growth in the West*, Allen and Unwin, 1964; S. J. Wells, *British Export Performance—A Comparative Study*, Cambridge University Press, 1964; Department of Economic Affairs, (D.E.A.), *Progress Reports* (Economic) nos. 1, 2 and 4, 1965, and Broadsheet no. 1, June 1965.

union policy. Now, of course, prices rise for various reasons: some specific, local, transitory; others as a consequence of fiscal (say, taxation) policy. In certain periods, as following the outbreak of the Korean War, the whole price level may be 'jacked up' under the impact of a great and sudden increase in demand. Nevertheless, it is generally held that the principal source of inflation in recent years is to be found on the side of costs or money incomes. Although probably no very sharp distinction between these 'demand-pull' and 'cost-push' explanations can be maintained in practice, it is clear that the most important single item in the selling price of our goods and services is constituted by money incomes, which comprise wages and salaries and also gross profits and other trading income. In 1963, for instance, money incomes accounted for almost three-quarters of the selling price of goods and services.[4] Now in the period 1953–63 money incomes increased on average by rather more than 6% a year, but the actual output of goods and services went up by little more than 2½% a year. That, ignoring our ability to put aside some of the output and to exchange it for imports on terms of varying degrees of advantage, was all we could dispose of, all we were entitled to. Yet under our silly arrangements we tried to take not 2½% a year but 6%. Naturally, under the magnet of that 'false' paper money, prices had to rise. Since the prices of our trade competitors did not rise to the same extent, imports were encouraged and our exports hindered. Hence adverse trade balances; hence recurrent balance-of-payments crises.

Where, then, does the responsibility—or irresponsibility—lie? Arguably, with the unions. For among the prices that rose was, of course, the price of labour, which means that labour costs were rising. Between 1953 and 1961 labour costs in Britain rose on average some 3% a year *faster* than the labour costs of our competitors.[5] In the two succeeding years, our relative cost position improved, but may have worsened again in 1964. In the meantime, the labour costs of many of our competitors remained more or less stable; in some instances, there seems to have been a fall. Accordingly it would not be surprising if, between 1953 and 1961, the export prices of British

[4] D.E.A. Broadsheet no. 1.

[5] D.E.A. *Progress Report* (Economic), no. 1.

manufactures had indeed gone up by 10% on average, compared with a 2% increase for German manufactures, and a fall, varying between 2% and 9%, in the export prices of French, Italian, Belgian and Japanese manufactures.[6] No doubt there are other factors: quality, delivery dates and the like. To be fluent, as distinct from being able to order a good dinner, in the language of one's potential customer would also help somewhat. Yet higher relative costs and prices seem to have constituted the most important single factor, or at least *a* major factor, in an export performance that, in terms of national needs, must be judged inadequate.

Now, it is the unions, so the argument runs, who are mainly responsible for those high relative costs and prices. True, in the period 1953–63, gross profits (and other trading income) increased by nearly 5½% on average, but wages and salaries went up by 6½%. Of the selling price of goods and services, whereas *gross* profits account for 23%, wages and salaries account for as much as 51% (in 1963). Wages and salaries, then, constituting the main component of selling prices, are forced up (it is said) by the unions, ruthlessly using their bargaining power in a period of full employment. Harassed by labour shortages, which have been generally very marked and often acute, employers feel compelled not only to hoard the skilled and semi-skilled workers they already have but even to give way to their unreasonable wage demands, both locally and nationally. This extra cost they pass on to consumers in the form of higher prices.

This, too, is a rather crude sketch, but it is plausible on historical grounds, there being ostensibly some association between levels of employment and increases in wages.[7] It is also just what Beveridge, in his advocacy of full employment, in a sense intended. For him the *point* of full employment was precisely to turn the labour market from a buyer's market into a seller's market. If a buyer of labour cannot buy—that is inconvenient; if a seller of labour cannot sell—that is disastrous. One might well judge, accordingly, that the unions have to bear a high degree of responsibility for our post-war trading

[6] Morgan Guaranty Trust *Survey*, July 1961, p. 7.

[7] See the work cited by Michael Stewart and Rex Winsbury, *An Incomes Policy for Labour*, Fabian Tract 350, Oct. 1963, pp. 22–3, n. 1.

difficulties in general and for our balance-of-payments crises in particular.

Even this very tentative conclusion will be angrily rejected by many trade unionists and not by them alone. In rebuttal they could argue that inflation was not the only source of balance-of-payments difficulties. In capital transactions, for example, British residents have, since 1952, invested abroad on average £150 millions *a year* more than foreigners have invested here. No doubt much of it came back as invisible earnings, but some of it might have been unnecessary or undesirable, or at least beyond our immediate capacity. *Invisibles* themselves deserve scrutiny. For about three generations *invisibles* took care of the adverse balance of (physical) *trade* that began to be normal towards the end of the last century. To-day, *invisibles* no longer discharge that historic role. Among several reasons for that, the relevant one is that the *invisibles* account, indeed the whole balance-of-payments account, has been dislocated by an item that was of no importance before the war: Government spending overseas, which has been as high as £300 millions a year. It covers overseas aid and particularly military expenditure abroad, which, it might be asserted, could and should have been kept down. Again, insofar as the balance-of-payments difficulties *were* due to inflation, one might plead not only that the employers were guilty too (gross profits being the other dynamic constituent of final prices) but also that successive Governments were at fault in failing to restrict the supply of money without which employers could not have met the unions' demands. So the counter-objections and recriminations might continue.

It is no part of my purpose, however, to weigh these (and other) arguments carefully in the balance. All I want is some 'operational' meaning for civic obligation that can be expressed in terms of union policy or behaviour. To that end I have tried to isolate an issue or problem which has been and remains of immense importance to the whole community, and for which—for its being a problem—the unions, *prima facie*, bear a heavy responsibility. Accepting, then, for arguments' sake, the criticism levelled at the unions, I suggest that they will be displaying civic virtue if they keep actual earnings within the annual increase in the output of goods and services, and specifically within the average annual rate of growth of 3.8% required by our 1965 National Plan for the period up to 1970. That is what we need as a community in order to achieve by 1970 a 25% increase in the output of goods and services, so essential for political and diplomatic as well as social purposes. If the unions do not keep actual earnings within the overall increase, they can be said to be acting irresponsibly.

In making a prognosis, we have first to recall that for actual earnings to be kept within the overall increase in productivity, the unions would have to exercise self-discipline at two distinct levels. In the first place, they would have to exercise wage restraint in national bargaining where the national basic-rate is set. This rate, however, is but a foundation for a complicated superstructure made up not only of payments made 'over the odds' (i.e. above the national rate) but also of several legitimate additional rates as well as of a special rate for piece-work. In mid-1964, for illustration, the national standard time-rate for an engineering fitter was £10 11s. 8d.; actual earnings were on average £16 for engineers on time-rates, without overtime. In manufacturing as a whole in 1959, it is estimated that the actual earnings, for a standard working week, were about a third higher than the standard rate and that the ratio was increasing.[8] In many an engineering factory, earnings are twice as high as wage rates.[9] Now the whole of this superstructure is erected by way of plant or workshop bargaining,[10] which accordingly constitutes the second level at which restraint would have to be exercised. If restraint is not exercised at the circumference, any restraint shown at the centre is undermined, actual earnings drifting away from the nationally-agreed basic rate. Not, indeed, that earnings-drift relates solely to increases in the basic-rate, which may remain unchanged while actual earnings drift away for other reasons (e.g., because men work more overtime, especially at week-ends). But this serves only to underline the importance of restraint at the second bargaining level. No doubt restraint should apply to local employers too,

[8] C. T. Saunders, 'Incomes Policy and Equity', Westminster Bank *Review*, Feb. 1965, pp. 6 and 7, no. 1.

[9] H. A. Clegg, 'Making an Incomes Policy Work', *Socialist Commentary*, Feb. 1965, p. 6.

[10] On workshop bargaining, see Arthur Marsh, *Managers and Shop Stewards*, Institute of Personnel Management, 1963.

but that is in a special sense of the term. Plagued by a persistent shortage of labour, especially skilled labour, they do add to earnings-drift by offering systematic overtime, paying 'over the odds' and the like. But I am assuming here that the onus is principally upon the unions. For, in a sense, the full-employment explanation does not explain enough. Full employment provides a bargaining opportunity; whether one exploits it irresponsibly depends on a certain wilful propensity to bargain. The point comes out well from H. A. Clegg's distinction between earnings-drift as a statistical conception and as a process—something that someone has to do *something about*[11]. That 'someone' is principally the union in the sense of the shop stewards, squeezing the last drop (critics might say) out of the bargaining opportunity provided by full employment, although individual members have a hand in the process insofar as they deliberately spread the work out during normal hours in order to 'earn' overtime. In a sense, earnings do not drift—they are levered.

At the national level the prospects for wage restraint are not bright. It is not only that, from the outset, the policy has been rejected by such significant unions as the Draughtsmen and the Transport and General Workers', the biggest union in the land and well represented in the engineering industry. (Engineering products account for something approaching a half of our exports, by value.) It is also that the unions whose executives voted for the policy in May, 1965 are not at all likely to exercise restraint except in the very short run. Their willingness even to declare themselves in favour of restraint is also too much dependent on the Labour Party's being in office to give one much confidence for the future. Above all, there are built-in forces operating inside the most well-intentioned unions that work against restraint. It is still too little realized that unions compete with one another in both political and social terms. Wage rates may be pushed up as a result of political rivalry between unions competing for membership or even between groups within a single union. 'Social' competition arises from notions of fairness, relative worth and status.[12]

[11] Ibid.

[12] A. M. Ross, *Trade Union Wage Policy*, University of California Press, 1956, and Barbara Wootton, *The Social Foundations of Wage Policy*, Allen and Unwin paperback, 1962; Allan Flanders, *Can Britain Have a Wage Policy?* roneod, 1958. Allan Flanders is one of the few to have emphasized these considerations.

Except in the short run, it is at present no use expecting the unions to display civic virtue in their national bargaining.

In workshop bargaining, even short-term restraint is scarcely conceivable. Union executive committees (and union annual conferences) may pass their resolutions but they are not in control of the shop stewards. Many factors (among them the two-tier structure of bargaining; the organization of trade unions, so many being represented in any one factory; the adoption by employers of payment-by-results, as well as full-employment itself) have combined, once again, to tip the balance of power in favour of the shop stewards, as against not only employers but also their own national union leaders. The national union leaders propose, but the shop stewards dispose—that is more or less the rule, at least where earnings-drift matters most to the community, i.e., in the engineering industry. Surely shop stewards, in general, will continue to exert themselves in workshop bargaining, in all probability screwing up earnings beyond the overall increase in productivity, with all that that implies for the community at large. Sooner rather than later, their example will be catching, and in due course, the incomes policy, if implemented at all, will be in ruins, and Britain, if not ruined, then weakened and in danger.

It is here that we reach the still neglected nub of incomes policy (as of much else in industrial relations). Earnings-drift has, of course, often been discussed in full-employment terms, but too often leaving the impression of some almost automatic process at work. It has been much less commonly remarked that earnings-drift is the result, in a given situation, of deliberate acts or choices by the shop stewards, responding for the most part to the wishes of the ordinary workers. Full employment provides the golden opportunity *but it need not be seized.* It is seized, not in general for ideological reasons (most shop stewards are neither Communists nor, probably, even Marxists), but because they have a certain propensity to bargain, which is an aspect of their character. The key to a successful incomes policy is to be found in the characters of the ordinary workers, from whom the shop stewards are drawn and to whom they (and in some degree the national union leaders) are responsive. Irresponsible they are, but that is because we have made them so in the industrial process, forgetting that factories produce men as well as goods.

It follows that one cannot rely in this discussion on the normal sociological method for explaining trade union action, which would be to show how and why it follows from a particular pattern of trade-union roles, which are 'bundles' of social norms (or expected actions) 'attached' to the various positions (general secretary, shop steward) in unions and supported by sanctions (rewards as well as punishments). For a sociologist, it is usually adequate to specify the norms, which, as Dahrendorf says, are then treated as axioms, not requiring further analysis.[13] But if we hope to influence union behaviour, we must know how union norms come to be what they are, and for that purpose we have to analyse the experience of men at their place of work. To think simply in terms of role-determined behaviour is, in any case, quite inadequate for the analysis of most practical problems. The social actions of a shop steward are indeed role-prescribed, as, for instance, in the union rule-book. But he also brings 'something' (personality, *self*, character) to the role. Institutional arrangements are, after all, mediated through individual human action.[14] Accordingly, we have to think of *interaction* between (roughly) character and role, not simply of the impact of role on behaviour.[15] To say this is not to imply 'psychologism' or 'reductionism', that is, reducing a sociological explanation to a psychological one. The sociologist is right to maintain that one cannot proceed directly from psychological properties (e.g. 'character') to social phenomena; too much happens 'in between', in 'the group situation'. It is simply a question of beginning at the beginning and not at the stage where, conventionally, the sociologist has chosen to enter.[16]

[13] In P. Laslett and W. G. Runciman (ed.), *Philosophy, Politics and Society*, 2nd series, Blackwell, 1962, p. 100.

[14] Cf. Alex Inkeles in Robert K. Merton, Leonard Broom and Leonard S. Cottrell, Jr. (ed.), *Sociology Today*, Basic Books, 1959, p. 251.

[15] Theodore R. Sarbin, in Gardner Lindzey (ed.), *Handbook of Social Psychology*, Addison Wesley, Reading, Mass., 1954, vol. I, p. 223.

[16] For practical problems, the division of labour between sociology and social psychology is distinctly odd. For a sensible reorganization, see Theodore M. Newcomb, 'Sociology and Psychology', in John Gillin (ed.), *For a Science of Social Man*, Macmillan, New York, 1954.

CHAPTER TWO

THE WORKERS' ROOT-NEEDS AND DISPOSITIONS

Introduction

That the individual workers arriving at the factory (a general term here for the larger commercial as well as industrial establishments) have certain fundamental needs, which I term root-needs, is a truism; until recently, however, it was one of those truisms that the social sciences had hardly outgrown. Even today, when innocently or in desperation, someone gives it currency, the only safe response is to nod one's head sagely, for it remains difficult to specify man's root-needs exactly—or even approximately. Since the 1890s at least, sociologists, social psychologists and plain seers have been compiling catalogues of needs in this particular sense.[1] Almost everything went into those catalogues but no general agreement has come out, partly because the cataloguers were cataloguing their own autobiographies.

Despair, however, would be premature. The composition as well as the fact of our bodily needs is the subject of almost universal agreement. Some social needs have been established by scientific (in the sense of experimental) procedures.[2] The existence of other needs, although not unsupported, is more speculative; even here, however, a converging tradition from both sides of the Atlantic embodies some valuable insights, and well serves the purpose in hand.

In this essay I can do no more than assert that the core of the tradition is necessity—the necessity of man's nature as a social being, expressing itself as his root-needs, in the classification of which the British sociologists Hobhouse and Ginsberg

[1] In the English-speaking world, the American sociologist Albion W. Small was perhaps the first to produce such a catalogue, which, under Germanic influence, he first drew up in 1893. See his *General Sociology*, University of Chicago Press, 1905.

[2] Michael Argyle, *Psychology and Social Problems*, Methuen, 1964, ch. 2.

virtually join hands with the American psychologists Maslow and Henry Murray. If I set aside the version I learned from Ginsberg in order to follow Maslow, it is partly because Maslow has written the more extensively and partly because his formulation has been persuasively applied to the industrial situation by the American psychologist, Douglas McGregor as well as by Maslow himself.[3] It is as well to emphasize that only part of what follows has been established by the methods of experimental psychology. It is true that there is more than one kind of scientific evidence: there is, for instance, clinical evidence, on which Maslow substantially relies. One must agree, however, that the Ginsberg-Maslow approach does have a 'humanist' as well as a scientific component, i.e. it rests in part upon insights from religion, philosophy and the great imaginative literature of the world. In defence one can suggest that there may be depths of human experience that are not amenable to the experimental method; one must resist the implied claim that what does not lend itself to that method is not important or does not even exist. In any case, in dealing with the great public issues we simply cannot wait until the last rat has devoured the last crumb: decisions have to be taken now on evidence that is obviously incomplete. However, the uncertainties must not be exaggerated. It is perfectly possible to reconcile a number of Maslow's 'needs' with those 'drives' accepted by so scientifically-minded a psychologist as Michael Argyle.[4]

It is also important to emphasize that there is no suggestion here of a fixed and unalterable list of needs; development is certainly possible, especially when a social group has been formed. What follows is simply a mode of exposition, a start having to be made somewhere. Finally, while allowance should

[3] L. T. Hobhouse, *Social Development*, Allen and Unwin, 1924, ch. VII; Morris Ginsberg's inaugural lecture 1930, in *Studies in Sociology*, Methuen, 1932, ch. VII, and his 1949–50 lectures in social philosophy at the London School of Economics; H. A. Murray *et al.*, *Explorations in Personality*, Oxford University Press, New York, 1938, and in T. Parsons and E. A. Shils, *Toward a General Theory of Action*, Harper Torchbooks, 1962, part 4, ch. 3; A. H. Maslow, *Motivation and Personality*, Harper and Row, 1954, and *Summer Notes on Social Psychology of Industry and Management*, Non-Linear Systems Inc., Del Mar. Calif., 1962; Douglas McGregor, *The Human Side of Enterprise*, McGraw-Hill, 1960.

[4] See note 2. This is my view. I have not asked either Argyle or Maslow for confirmation.

be made for differences between cultures, it seems that factory problems in Britain and the United States have much in common.[5] Accordingly, I draw upon research done on both sides of the Atlantic.

* * * * *

It is convenient to visualize the workers as young school-leavers making a start in a newly-established factory in some fairly remote district with weak trade-union traditions. When they arrive at the gates, they will be presenting not only their physical persons but also as many selves, or psychological entities or constructs, in which a major element will be their root-needs.[6] Doubtless no one institution could be held responsible for meeting the whole range of human needs; yet some needs are 'indivisible'. If a need for food can be satisfied off the job through the device of wages, it would seem impossible to confine a need for 'belongingness' to a man's leisure or off-duty hours. It is an on-duty, on-going need—it cannot be compartmentalized, suppressed from eight to five and then given rein as the workers come trooping out on to the road. And more generally, a factory is not just another institution. In our culture one's job is a defining characteristic, and so one strives to satisfy one's needs to the full at one's place of work.

What, then, are the root-needs of these young workers? It is usual to sort their root-needs, which are aspects of their characters, into two boxes, for which the labels *biogenic* and *sociogenic* are as convenient as any.[7] Biogenic needs comprise, for example, the need for oxygen, without which the cells of the brain suffer irreparable damage within two or three minutes; after the lapse of another two or three minutes, we leave all needs far behind. Water and food, of course, come under this heading. Without water we might see the week out in a

[5] See Chris Argyris, *Personality and Organization*, Harper, 1957, pp. 161 and 271, for the view of two experienced American observers that in the U.S.A., England, parts of Western Europe and Scandinavia, problems within the plant are much the same.

[6] Maslow's term is *basic needs*, which was Ginsberg's too in his 1949–50 lectures. But I have become accustomed to *root-needs*, my variant of Hobhouse's and the earlier Ginsberg's *root-interests*, also to *self-fulfilment* or *self-realization* rather than *self-actualization*.

[7] Muzafer Sherif, *An Outline of Social Psychology*, Harper, 1948, Part One. The corresponding *concepts*, however, are not identical with those used here.

temperate climate; in a hot climate we would do well to last out a day. The need for food includes particular forms of intake. The tragic death of the American child whose craving for salt had been gratified at home but, in ignorance, not at the hospital to which it had been admitted for some routine purpose, is a reminder of the thirty or so substances we must eat to live. At home the child had literally been eating salt to live. Other needs, such as the sexual, are almost as insistent, even if, contrary to the oral tradition among schoolboys and youths, the failure to acheive gratification does not actually cause death.

To turn to the sociogenic needs is to step off firm ground on to shifting sands. Casting one's net to bring in clinical and other 'broad' evidence, one first catches a root-need for safety—for a fairly stable, orderly, manageable *social* environment. (As *control* is perhaps the central notion here, this need would seem to approximate to Argyle's need for *power*.) In itself the need for safety is thought to be not inconsistent with some risk-taking unless men feel threatened or dependent. If they do feel so, as in at least some factories, this need will tend to embrace protection against danger, threat and deprivation.

There follows a root-need for love and affection, giving as well as receiving, or, more broadly, a root-need to belong. (This corresponds exactly to Argyle's *affiliative need*). In its wake comes a root-need for esteem, or respect. This may have two elements: self-respect and the deserved respect of others. One finds no exact correspondence here with the scientific canon, but Argyle, discussing human problems in industry, does take note of 'recognition in their work' as a factor contributing to men's very high job satisfaction.[8] It is possible, too, that W. H. Scott's elucidation of the general connection between high status and high morale has some bearing on this need for esteem.[9]

Crowning all, and possibly subsuming all, there is perhaps a root-need for self-realization, or self-fulfilment—including the need to do what one is fitted for, to crystallize what is potential within us. It could well be expressed in the terms that Isaiah Berlin used to discuss the positive conception of freedom:

[8] Argyle, op. cit., p. 108.

[9] W. H. Scott, et al., *Coal and Conflict*, Liverpool University Press, 1963, p. 182.

> 'I wish to be somebody, not nobody; a doer—deciding, not being decided for, self-directed and not acted upon by external nature or by other men as if I were a thing, or an animal, or a slave incapable of playing a human role, that is, of conceiving goals and policies of my own and realizing them.'[10]

Conceiving goals of my own and realizing them: that catches the spirit of the need for self-realization or self-fulfilment. Here again nothing exactly like this can be found in the scientific canon, but Argyle noted that when men achieved success or recognition in their work (and so felt particularly high satisfaction), they experienced it as 'personal growth or self-realization'.[11] A need for achievement, however, is well attested by the scientists,[12] and that bears very closely upon self-realization.

In short, sufficient convergence exists, I believe, between differing traditions and approaches to permit one to say that the sociogenic needs are made up of the needs for safety (or power); affection (the affiliative); esteem (or respect, recognition); and self-realization (or, in part, achievement). Counting the biogenic, one may provisionally suggest that the fundamental needs of Anglo-American man fall into roughly five broad classes.

Maslow and McGregor, however, go farther than that: they believe that these fundamental needs are arranged in sequence (in the order in which I have introduced them) and hierarchically, the affiliative need, for example, being 'higher' than the need for safety, the need for self-realization being the highest of all. The idea of a sequence is essentially that of each class of need's standing like a sentry and barring access to a series of inner camps or compounds until the proper password has been given. That password is 'relative satisfaction'. Otherwise put, unless the biogenic needs are relatively (=partially) satisfied,

[10] Isaiah Berlin, *Two Concepts of Liberty*, Clarendon Press, Oxford, 1958, p. 16.

[11] ibid.

[12] Argyle, op. cit., ch. 2, and David C. McClelland, *The Achieving Society*, Van Nostrand, 1961. A convenient source for McClelland's ideas about achievement drive and economic growth is *The Roots of Consciousness*, Van Nostrand Insight Book (paperback), 1964, ch. 2. On the significance of the achievement need for the quality of a social group's (or institution's) functioning, i.e., its significance for what character or personality brings to the role, see Alex Inkeles, op. cit. (n. 14 above), pp. 264–6.

a man cannot proceed to the next stage, where he will be actuated by the need for safety. A man's life will then be dominated by his biogenic needs; a man barely able to satisfy his hunger, for instance, *does* tend, as Maslow observes, to live by bread alone. Indeed, where social organization has failed (as in pre-war South Wales, where in some towns eight or nine men out of ten were unemployed, or West Virginia), the 'higher'[13] needs may atrophy for want of satisfaction, as in other, still less favoured lands where whole peoples live on the margin of subsistence, such needs, judging by the absence of the literary and visual arts, may not even appear.

On the other hand, once the biogenic needs have been relatively satisfied, the original pressure subsides (for the time being), leaving the path open for the safety need to exert itself. This in turn yields, after being relatively satisfied, to the pressure deriving from the affiliative need. At a 'higher' level still, the need for esteem waits to be aroused. Only when it has been partially satisfied will a man enjoy that kind of freedom in which he can live a creative, constructive (i.e. self-fulfilling) life.

This sequence is not thought to hold good for every man. Structurally, the need for esteem or respect may take precedence in some persons over the need for love. In the religious genius, on the other hand, the need for love is overflowing and overwhelming. In terms of 'flow', or dynamic sequence, the struggling artist in his garret may sustain a highly creative (=self-fulfilling) life on a diet of bread and brandy or even bread and water. The Roman Catholic priest is celibate; in the extreme case, the holy man lies, half-starved, on his bed of nails. These are exceptions, however, to the usual pattern.

[13] The terms 'higher' and 'lower' contain complexities. As between the biogenic and the sociogenic, 'lower' may be taken to mean 'more essential for sheer survival'. But when it comes to precedence between sociogenic categories, say belongingness and esteem, we cannot use such a distinction. 'Lower' might then mean: in the evolutionary sense. Those needs would be lowest which we shared with all organisms; one could then visualize a sort of sliding-scale rising from organisms, to animals, to mammals, to primates, to humans. 'Higher' would thus come to mean 'more human'. Needs may also be said to be 'higher' in the sense of developmental psychology: the infant shows only physiological or biogenic needs, the other needs appearing only in succession. Needs are also higher in that their satisfaction contributes not merely to survival but survival on certain highly valued terms: one not only lives but lives bright-eyed, alert, sleeping well, free from chronic illness. This quality of living is attained when the self-fulfilling need is satisfied. See Maslow, *Motivation and Personality*, ch. 8.

It must be said, however, that this idea of a sequence and hierarchy is but a working hypothesis. The scientific or experimental psychologist is content at present to isolate needs and not to set out their relationship (if any). It would be perfectly possible to sustain my argument on the basis of the three well-established needs (for power, love, achievement), and scientists may reconstruct accordingly. The thesis would then turn, as we shall see, on the frustration of these three needs in the factory, no attempt being made to place them in order of importance. If I go farther, it is partly because Maslow 'speaks to' my own experience of three large-scale organizations, and because when applied to the industrial situation, his idea is, I think, illuminating.

Whether using Maslow's schema or that of other psychologists, we have to grasp the strength of the sociogenic needs. It is easy, especially if thinking in terms of precedence, to assume that the sociogenic needs are somehow less important than the biogenic ones, which indeed one is tempted to conceive of as serviced by the former. But it is arguable that the distinction between biogenic and sociogenic does not correspond exactly to that between innate and learned. In other words, some root-needs called sociogenic and seemingly acquired or learned may be innate, e.g. the affiliative need. Many psychologists would deny it, preferring to explain the affiliative need as in some way derivative—from the baby's helplessness after birth, from the prolonged period of breast-feeding, from the affection felt by the baby for its mother, from the reward (e.g. a reduction in anxiety) gained in infancy from affiliative behaviour itself,[14] or in other ways. In questioning (in good company) these interpretations, one is not falling back on the simple postulate of 'gregarious instincts'[15] but rather taking account of what is

[14] For one or other of these explanations, see, e.g., D. W. Harding, *Social Psychology and Individual Values*, Hutchinson, 1952, p. 11, and J. A. C. Brown, *The Social Psychology of Industry*, Penguin Books, 1954, p. 281.

[15] That revulsion against instincts which was so marked a feature of the intellectual scene after 1919–20 was no doubt overdue. When thousands of alleged instincts come to be reported, including even an instinct for licking sugar, and when instincts are regarded as immutable, it is time for a typhoon, not a mere wind, of change to blow. Like so many sharp intellectual changes in direction, this one went too far. So long as one does not neglect the phenomenon of the fusion of root-needs or the plasticity of 'matching' forms and modes of action, which are widely held to be learned behaviour, or assume that innate dispositions are

actually known about the primates—man and his nearest living relatives in the animal kingdom. In their natural state, all anthropoid apes show a capacity at least for family life, while some show a capacity for group life generally.[16] In general, too, when they move about in bands in the wild state, they show little friction and much sociability. Between primates of the same sex, lasting friendships have been observed, in which they sit and rest together, and even groom each other's coats in mutual affection.[17] In captivity, chimpanzees show a capacity for friendship and are upset and unhappy when an established friend is taken away, even if they are not then left alone. Altruism, a disinterested concern for others, can be discerned in the higher mammals.[18] No doubt these observations would carry more weight if we could still think in terms of a straight-line development from the precursors of such present-day primates to man instead of probably having to recognize the early separation of their evolutionary lines. Even so, the observations, especially of social behaviour in the wild state, carry some weight. If we add that man himself is obviously social now and may, on the evidence of fossils, have been social for several million years,[19] then it is far from rash to conclude with the English psychologist, D. W. Harding, and others, that the social (or affiliative) impulse is innate.[20] Again, if the need for self-fulfilment can be opened like a parasol to cover curiosity, novelty, intellectual exploration, problem-solving, mild risk-taking and some excitement, then some part of it at least may be innate in man as a mammal.[21]

mysterious entities or 'little men' inside us rather than mechanisms that the physiologist will one day explain, it seems unnecessary to offer a blanket opposition to the very idea of innateness to account at least for some of men's needs other than the biogenic. It seems wiser, in fact, to examine the evidence.

[16] Marston Bates, 'Human Ecology', in A. L. Kroeber (ed.), *Anthropology Today*, University of Chicago, fifth impression, 1958, p. 708.

[17] W. M. S. Russell, *The Listener*, 5 Nov. 1964.

[18] D. O. Hebb and W. R. Thompson, 'The Social Significance of Animal Studies', in Gardner Lindzey (ed.), op. cit.

[19] Marston Bates, ibid.

[20] Harding, ibid. Talcott Parsons and Edward A. Shils (ed.), *Toward A General Theory of Action*, Harper Torchbooks, 1962, p. 9, allow that the need for social relationships may be 'constitutionally given'.

[21] Hebb and Thompson, ibid.: W. I. Walker and R. Cattell, quoted in David Krech, Richard C. Crutchfield and Egerton L. Ballachey, *Individual in Society*, McGraw-Hill, 1962, p. 99; Maslow, *Motivation and Personality*, pp. 92–3. Even

Now, if some of the needs called sociogenic are in fact innate, their satisfaction must be in some sense as important as the satisfaction of the biogenic, which is easily overlooked because we see so vividly the sense in which the biogenic needs (such as the need for oxygen) must take precedence. If, on the other hand, we fail to satisfy, for instance, the affiliative need, we survive—but only at the cost of doing violence to our nature. Even those psychologists who deny the innateness of the affiliative need and see it as somehow derivative do not deny its profound importance in its own right. It is even possible, on occasion, for the sociogenic needs to supplant the biogenic. To survive is doubtless the normal objective; yet men are not always prepared to survive on *any* terms. 'Death before dishonour' is no Blimpish cry. The need for esteem may be so strong that suicide is preferred to public disgrace—the knowing looks, the clack of tongues. The need for achievement may drive a man into a way of life that ruins his health, a result symbolized by the company director's ulcers and the scholar's fading eyesight.

None of these root-needs, biogenic or sociogenic, should be confused with the specific desires that appear daily on the conscious 'screens' of our minds. Such desires are but 'coloured markers' pointing to the deep-set needs of which men are likely to be only partly or even wholly unconscious. How, then, can root-needs be identified? Inferences can be drawn from observed behaviour; a man who spends much time in social activities may be judged, *provisionally*, to have a strong affiliative need. Projective techniques can be used. These range from the Rorschach ink-blot test (named after the Swiss psychologist) and various other 'picture' tests to word-association and sentence-completion exercises. 'Picture' tests are particularly relevant to our inquiry. In these, one is essentially presented with an ambiguous or 'unstructured' stimulus, such as an ink-blot or a vague picture, and one is then required to 'make something of it'. In the process of making something of it, such as telling a story suggested by the stimulating object, people are presumed to reveal, among other things, their

psychologists who generally use learning theory to account for the sociogenic needs tend to see the curiosity need as 'biologically deep-rooted'. See, e.g., David Krech, et al., ibid.

deepest needs. David McClelland, the Harvard psychologist, has adapted one of these techniques in a way very much to our purpose. In some people, the picture he used (a man at a workbench on which stands a small family photograph) evoked stories redolent of pleasant family occasions, past or prospective. In other respondents, the picture evoked stories embodying a plan of action, with a brief indication of the problems likely to be encountered in carrying out the plan, the method of overcoming them, and the final, individual decision. These images suggested a powerful need for achievement.[22]

If root-needs are not specific desires, what is the relationship between them? It is certainly complex. In general it will not be 'one-to-one', a specific desire symmetrically matching one root-need. On the contrary, one specific desire may serve several root-needs. Thus a particular sexual impulse may meet not only a need for 'release of tension' (which we may suppose here to be a component of the biogenic root-needs) but also the affiliative need and even the root-need for esteem, since in some societies (? Paris) the successful womanizer is regarded as a high achiever of a kind. Similarly, a wage-claim, especially for the restoration of differentials between craftsmen and the semi-skilled, may have as much to do with the root-need for esteem as with the standard of living. Looked at from the vantage-point of the root-needs themselves, this is the phenomenon called 'fusion': the biogenic need (served by wages)

[22] McClelland, *The Roots of Consciousness*, ch. 2. That needs are so deep-set as to require this kind of discovery goes some way to countering R. S. Peters's criticism of the needs approach, especially Maslow's. (*The Concept of Motivation*, Routledge and Kegan Paul, 1958, esp. pp. 134–5). Anticipating the psychologist's counter-argument that terms like 'drive' and 'need' are strictly technical, Peters answers that the different terms used by ordinary educated people incorporate distinctions that psychologists must not ignore, and that common-sense, embodied in ordinary language, has already 'creamed off' most of the vital distinctions in psychology. (pp. 154–5). This can hardly be so if people are even partly unaware of their needs. One wonders generally whether Peters is not guilty of what Frederick Bodmer called the 'belief that accepted habits of expression among European nations are connected with universal principles of reasoning'. (*The Loom of Language*, Allen and Unwin, 1946, p. 132). Some of the best educated men in the Middle Ages thought that the verb *to be* denoted real existence even when used to call attention to some attribute of a person or thing. For instance, if one can say 'Such views are false', there *must* be in the realm of *Ideas* a substance called *falsity*. Even educated common sense had failed to distinguish between different functions of the verb *to be*. Similarly, the educated non-specialist may have missed some distinctions that the specialist (in this case, the psychologist) can bring to light.

fuses with the esteem need to produce the specific desire embodied in a wage claim. Looked at from the other end, it is a specific desire fanning out to meet two needs. On the other hand, although some root-needs require specific service, others do not and so can be at least partly gratified in two or even more ways. Thus hunger (an element of course in the biogenic needs) may be served by smoking as well as food. Here one root-need fans out into a number of specific desires or actions.

Neither specific desire nor root-need should be visualized as isolated entities within us—mainsprings or 'little men' directing our behaviour. 'Springs' psychology—the reduction of human nature to certain basic experiences or impulses, as in the work of the seventeenth-century philosopher-mathematicians, Descartes and Hobbes—has long been discredited, intellectually if not in the world of industry, which it reached somewhere during the course of the Industrial Revolution, the hard-bottomed men who made it being Cartesians to a man. As against 'instincts' (a species of 'springs' psychology), the philosopher John Laird criticized long ago the assumption of 'occult qualities' within us. By coincidence or as an unconscious echo of Laird, the Oxford philosopher Gilbert Ryle, in a related discussion, has spoken up against the presumption of 'ghostly' or 'occult' thrusts inside us.[23] In the discussion of industrial behaviour that follows I have tried to keep to what I believe to be Ryle's point—that the explanation of a person's behaviour shall be couched in terms of his character or disposition.[24] If I give an impression of resorting to 'springs' psychology, it is because of the difficulty of avoiding it; as the English psychologist-sociologist, W. J. H. Sprott, has observed, the usual psychological models still conceive of persons in terms of a 'ghost in the machine'—with desires (=needs) and values which, by the use of reason, they try to actualize.[25] Even more I have suffered from the difficulty of having to make analytical distinctions of a type that threaten to distort the unity of men's characters or personalities. Root-needs, then, are not

[23] Laird, *Idea of Value*, quoted in Ginsberg, *Studies in Sociology*, p. 123, and Gilbert Ryle, *The Concept of Mind*, Hutchinson's University Library, 1949, pp. 64, 65, 67, 110.

[24] pp. 43, 45, 88–92, 106.

[25] *Social Psychology*, Methuen, 1952, pp. 7–8.

little men within us, swimming about inside, superior tadpoles of the mind (or somewhere): they are embedded in character, properties of men, and extracted with some violence only to meet the exigencies of exposition. The rest of the book, in fact, is an attempt to disclose how the characters or dispositions of the workers, and hence of trade unionists, are formed, and how if we will, these can be changed.

But, it may be objected, are not their characters (or personalities) formed in infancy and early childhood? That character is *fully* formed in *infancy* (say, the first twelve months) seems to be no more than a vulgarization of Freud, but what of the view that it is *basically* formed in early childhood? These are deep waters, but the view I have, for better or worse, adopted is that the correct Freudian, or perhaps neo-Freudian, position is merely that child personality *provides a framework for* adult personality. Expressed in terms of learning, as, for instance, by Geoffrey Gorer, early learning (or habit) influences all subsequent learning.[26] Thus the young school-leavers arrive at the factory with characters-in-outline that are unique to individuals and yet bear a strong family resemblance in respect of root-needs. The 'reception' of those needs in the factory rounds off the young men's characters. Looking back to our starting-point, we begin to penetrate the deep pools of Maslow's aphorism: 'When we ask what man wants of life, we deal with his very essence,'[27]

[26] Quoted in Alex Inkeles and David J. Levinson in Gardner Lindzey, (ed.) op. cit., vol. II, pp. 999–1000. I have followed them.

[27] Maslow, *Motivation and Personality*, p. 106.

CHAPTER THREE

THE IDEA OF A FACTORY

The young workers arrive, then, at the factory, where, or at another like it, most of them will remain for thirty or forty years. How far will the factory environment prove congenial to the gratification of their needs? It is a very difficult question to answer. Researchers have for the most part so neglected the close study of the structure and actual functioning of factories that few empirical generalizations can be safely made about one of the central institutions of our time.[1] In the absence of empirical generalizations of the relevant kind, I am compelled to adopt a special procedure. I first ask: what, for the purpose of this inquiry, is, as it were, the *minimum idea* of a factory, whether at Dagenham or Dortmund, Detroit or Dnepropetrovsk? From the answer to that question I can draw certain inferences. These should, of course, be checked on the ground, but as that cannot be attempted here, they will have to be treated as plausible generalizations. I shall then be in a position, in the next chapter, to suggest the probable outcome of the 'confrontation' between workers' needs and the factory environment. Treating that outcome as a hypothesis, I shall proceed to ask what empirical evidence bears upon it.

What characterizes a factory (in the extended sense in which I use that term throughout)? I begin with the platitude that the work to be done is not merely divided but sub-divided: Marx called it *the division of labour in detail*.[2] Now the broader division of labour in society at large is presumably as old as civilization itself—some different work for different hands even in simple agriculture; trading as distinct from agriculture and primitive industry; the various branches of even primitive industry. But the sub-division of labour under the same roof,

[1] Cf. Norman C. Hunt (Edinburgh), *The Listener*, 2 Oct. 1958.

[2] *Capital*, vol. 1, Everyman's ed. 1942, p. 270.

as in Adam Smith's famous example of the making of one part of a pin, was a startling new development in social organization. Today, in factories in the narrower sense, the method has of course been carried very much farther. In many of these the operations are mechanized, some in the form of an assembly line. In others (an increasing number) the operations are automated, i.e. made self-correcting through an electronic 'feed-back' device. Even in other types of establishment than the factory proper, including the larger commercial offices, the work is considerably sub-divided and increasingly mechanized. Factory work is finely subdivided work.

From this we can infer that sub-division requires at least one sub-divider. The duties and correlative rights (or social norms) of each sub-divided position (works manager, foreman, operative) have to be defined with varying degrees of explicitness; the larger the factory, the greater the explicitness, possibly necessitating a written document or at least some written instructions. Apart from specific instructions, the social norms (which, bundled together, constitute a social role corresponding to each position) have to enjoin impersonal and impartial treatment all round: customers, clients and even other employees are to be treated more as 'cases' or cogs than as persons in their own right if the end result of the work is to be efficiently achieved. Position is to interact with position rather than person with person, emotional attachments being, in principle, foregone for the duration of the working day. To ensure that social roles are carried out as intended (or at least to keep variations within acceptable bounds), each matching position will have to be equipped with a set of sanctions, i.e. rewards and punishments. Above all, the implication from first to last is that a structure of authority will be indispensable: planning, defining, co-ordinating, sanctioning, *and* continuous adjustment to changing objectives and circumstances—all seem to require a hierarchical differentiation of positions, their occupants being related as superior to subordinate. The works manager, necessarily subordinate to the managing director, is necessarily superior to the workers at the bench.

Thus the defining characteristic of a factory (the division of labour in detail) seems necessarily to entail another characteristic—superiority and subordination. Authority is at the core of the idea of a factory. This is another of those commonplaces that ought to be marked by buoys and warning lights. The crucial error, of course, in both Marx and John Stuart Mill, although not in Marx's collaborator, Engels, was to see authority in terms of ownership. Setting out from the division of labour in detail, Marx saw a factory as an army. Like a general on the battlefield (Marx wrote), the capitalist commands in the field of production, assisted by commissioned officers (the managers) and non-commissioned officers (the foremen and overlookers). The emphasis on *command*, a term which Marx uses in several passages, is no doubt appropriate; *who says factory, says command.* That, however, is my formula, not Marx's. For him, command in industry was essentially an attribute of capital, as, under feudalism, command in war had been an attribute of landed property. The capitalist is not a capitalist because he is a commander of industry; he becomes a commander of industry because he is a capitalist.[3] The division of labour in detail is a development peculiar to the capitalist method of production. The manufacturing division of labour makes it a technical necessity to increase the number of workers under a unit of *capital*; manufacture does not merely subject the formerly independent worker to the control and discipline of *capital*, but, in addition, it creates a hierarchical gradation among the 'workers themselves'.[4]

A generation earlier, in 1848, when Marx published his famous pamphlet the *Communist Manifesto*, the Liberal economist and philosopher, John Stuart Mill had made that same identification of authority with capital ownership. He saw the workers as 'mere servants under the *command* of the one *who supplies* the funds';[5] and he bravely set out to heal 'the widening and embittering feud between the class of labourers and the class of *capitalists*'.[6] His remedy, of course, was poles apart from Marx's; he was one of the early advocates of partnership in industry. But, in this particular respect, his diagnosis was much the same. And for good reason: industrial evolution had actually

[3] ibid., pp. 348–9.

[4] ibid., pp. 370–81. Italics added.

[5] *Principles of Political Economy*, John W. Parker, London, 1848, vol. II, ch. VII, pp. 323–4.

[6] ibid., p. 332.

brought about such a conjunction or identification. From medieval times to the eighteenth century, we had passed (schematically expressed) through two phases. The first had been the family or household system, essentially an at-home arrangement in which there was virtually no market. It was superseded by the gild or handicrafts system, in which a division of labour by crafts occurred. Craftsmen such as smiths and weavers might still have small holdings, but they worked primarily at their craft, either at the customer's home or at their own. The materials were their own or were supplied by the customer. Between producer and consumer, there was no intermediary; the master craftsman was the dealer, the market small and localized. If one could speak of employer and employed, relations were patriarchal. The succeeding domestic system was characterized by a widening market, in which a middleman came to be interposed between producer and consumer. The middleman provided the materials to be worked up and found the market for the product. But the worker (the producer) was not necessarily divorced from his working tools (or instruments of production): these he might retain as his own property or under lease from the middleman. In either case, he would use them at home (hence, of course, 'domestic').[7] The factory system that followed presents, of course, a profoundly important development. In this system the market has widened and become far more complex; more expensive machinery has been introduced, which the ordinary man cannot afford. Accordingly he loses control not only of the materials to work on but also of the instruments to work on the materials. A wide social cleavage between employer and employed begins to emerge, symbolized by the appearance of trade unions. Production is more and more divided 'in detail' and on a larger scale. Thus everything conspires to force the worker (producer) out of his home to congregate under one roof. The owner or controller of the capital required for all these developments now not only finds the market but also regulates the manufacture, which is a new function in history.[8] Patriarchal attitudes begin to decline.

[7] W. J. Ashley, *The Economic Organization of England*, new ed. with additional chapter by G. C. Allen, Longmans, 1935, esp. lecture VII.

[8] ibid., p. 154.

All this Marx and Mill could see from their mid-century vantage point; the crucial change by which the owner or controller of the capital had come to direct and supervise the manufacturing process took place, as a characteristic feature, during the latter years of the previous century.[9] We, living in the post-nationalization period, have no such defence. To us it ought to be obvious that command in industry has survived the partial and even the complete extinction of the capitalist. How far ownership has been divorced from command is still uncertain; the only certainty is that James Burnham's 'managerial revolution'[10] grossly exaggerated the extent of it. In the average large company both in this country and the United States, it seems likely, after all, that ultimate decision-making still remains with the largest capital shareholders. More specifically, at least a quarter of the very large companies with capital of over £3 million (in 1951) are thought to have been controlled directly or indirectly, by the large shareholders.[11] Burnham took a powerful trend and turned it into a completed process. No one doubts, however, that such a trend, deriving very largely from the Limited Liability Act of 1854 and the consequential wider dispersion of share (and hence factory) ownership, is at work. It ought therefore to be plain that command depends not on ownership but on the division of labour in detail. This dependence is most strikingly demonstrated where private industry has been nationalized. The command structure of a nationalized industry is, in essentials, no whit different from that of private industry, hedged about though it invariably is by the trappings of constitutionalism (as in the form of joint consultation). It is at last plain to see that capitalism in industry is one thing, command in industry quite another.

That this was plain to Engels if not to Marx himself is even now not generally realized. Writing in an obscure Italian revolutionary journal in 1874, Engels discussed this very question of authority in the factory, and specifically whether it

[9] ibid.

[10] *The Managerial Revolution*, Putnam, 1942.

[11] P. Sargant Florence, *The Logic of British and American Industry*, Routledge and Kegan Paul, rev. ed. 1961, Part V, and 'Measuring Shareholders' Control' in *The Times*, 12 Aug. 1959.

could be dispensed with under a different social system.[12] His answer was a forceful 'No'. Modern industry, he argued, entailed more and more combined action, especially in the mechanized form. But that meant organization: could there be organization without authority? If a social revolution overthrew the capitalists now exercising authority, would authority be overthrown too? No; the 'authority of the steam' would remain; the automatic machinery of a big factory would prove to be far more despotic than any small capitalist had ever been. To keep the wheels turning, the worker would have to subordinate himself to decisions taken by 'a dominant', some elected committee perhaps but possibly even a single person. Over the entrance to the factory during working hours, this injunction ought to be written—

Lasciate ogni autonomia, voi che entrate!

This has been translated as: *Leave, ye that enter in, all autonomy behind!*[13] But that quite fails to catch the overtones of the line, which, of course, echoes Dante, whom Marx himself liked to quote:

Lasciate ogni speranza voi ch'entrate

Appearing over the entrance to the *Inferno*, this has been traditionally translated as:

Abandon all hope, ye who enter here

It is that sense of 'abandon all hope of autonomy in the factory' that Engels, surely, meant to convey.

I deduce, then, that the idea of a factory, nationalized or privately-owned, is the idea of command. How far does this inference find support in the articulated experience of men who have actually managed large-scale enterprises? A review of the literature would, I believe, furnish substantial support. Here I can only bring to bear the reflections of Henri Fayol, the French mining engineer who turned so successfully to industrial

[12] Lewis S. Feuer (ed.), *Marx and Engels: Basic Writings*, Doubleday Anchor, 1959, pp. 481–4, 'On Authority', which was drawn to my attention by Professor Seymour M. Lipset.

[13] ibid.

management.[14] Looking back over a lifetime of practical experience, Fayol, like Woodrow Wilson, enunciated fourteen points or principles; he also subjected to analysis the managerial process itself as he had experienced it. Now 'principles' of management are often ambiguous and even vacuous, as three leading American authorities make plain in their scathing dismissal of the principles rashly set out by a former vice-president of General Motors.[15] But my concern here is not at all with managerial or administrative theory as such. It is true that Fayol's principles are recommendations to action, but their basis is not a mechanistic theory of man as a mere tool or instrument but rather Fayol's own experience of what the managing of a large-scale enterprise entails. Like his analysis of the managerial process, his principles, although hortatory in form, may well be read as empirical generalizations.

The fourteen points need not be enumerated[16]; Fayol's general view is that the technical requirements of production demand an extensive division of labour, which in turn demands great co-ordination. Authority and its corollary responsibility thus come to occupy a central place in the factory scheme of things. This authority should be concentrated rather than diffused; should confer unity of direction, plans being dovetailed together in order to achieve the overriding objectives of the factory; should be hierarchically arranged, instructions being passed down the line from superior to subordinate in such a way as to maintain discipline and also unity of command,

[14] Fayol (1841–1925) became a colliery manager in France and later general manager of a great coal and metallurgical company there. The company was on its last legs when he took over in 1888, but he pulled it through and built up a highly successful concern. The lectures outlining his ideas were given in 1900 and 1908, although his book (*Administration industrielle et Générale*) was not published until 1916. An English translation of a later edition was published in Geneva in 1925 by the International Institute of Management, and in London in 1949 by Pitman's. Fayol influenced several outstanding management theorists, including the American Luther Gulick and the Englishman, Lyn Urwick.

[15] James G. March, Herbert A. Simon and Harold Guetkow, *Organization*, Wiley, 3rd Printing 1961, p. 30. Vice-President Mooney's article can be found in L. Gulick and L. Urwick, *Papers on the Science of Administration*, Institute of Public Administration, Columbia University, New York, 1937, pp. 89–98.

[16] Division of work; authority and responsibility; discipline; unity of command; unity of direction; subordination of individual interest to general interest; remuneration to personnel; centralization; scalar chain; order; equity; stability of tenure of personnel; initiative; *esprit de corps*.

each subordinate receiving instructions from no more than one superior. But this 'unity of command' is no mere imposition; it turns in part upon *esprit de corps* and on fair dealing by managers. Nor are subordinates to be treated as 'living automatons' (the Scottish philosopher, Dugald Stewart's term for manufacturing workers); they should be given the chance to exercise initiative, one of the keenest of satisfactions for intelligent men.

The theme of command recurs, too, in Fayol's analysis of the managerial process. In this the first stage is occupied by *prévoyance*: looking ahead, judging the future and making provision for it. Out of that comes a plan, which defines the objectives, the line of action to be pursued, the stages to be traversed and the methods to be used. Given the plan, managers have to establish the human and material relationships to attain it; in Fayol's sense, they have to organize. In so doing, they command their subordinates and co-ordinate their activities. Finally, the plan has to be verified in order to see that it is being adhered to: this is control, backed by sanctions.

Thus the practical manager, Fayol, articulating his own long experience, reaches (up to a point) much the same conception of the nature of a factory as the social theorist, Marx—one of those improbable conjunctions in the history of ideas until it is recalled that Marx the social theorist is also Marx the industrial analyst and historian. And this way of thinking about the nature of a factory is implied in the work of some British management theorists with experience of industry and business.[17] Thus what experienced managers have said about the actual nature of management accords with the conception of the nature of a factory which can be deduced from the mere *fact* of the division of labour in detail. The inference we drew (in the absence of suitable generalizations about actual factories) is sufficiently validated (or at least encouraged) for the argument to proceed.

But, it may be asked, need the argument have been held up? Is not all perfectly obvious? The answer is that the idea of a

[17] See, for example, L. Urwick, *The Function of Administration*, in Gulick and Urwick, op. cit., pp. 115–30, and Ernest E. Butten, at the relevant time, Chairman of Personnel Administration Ltd., 'Management and Organization', National Provincial Bank *Review*, May 1957, p. 7.

factory as command is now challenged in the debate between 'mechanistic' and 'organismic' theories of organization (and of management). One cannot deny that Fayol contributed to what is now identifiable as the classical theory of organization, which crystallized in the years before the First World War. Fayol's ideas were first aired in lectures in 1900 and 1908, but apparently did not gain much attention then. The classical theory is really a compound, seemingly unrelated at the time, of the scientific management theories of the American engineer, Frederick Taylor, whose main work was published in 1911, and the theory of bureaucracy formulated by the German sociologist, Max Weber, in 1911–13, although not published until some years later, by which time Fayol's book was also available. In their very different modes, they (and many others) did tend to think 'mechanistically', embodying or implying in their theories and plans a conception of man as a mere machine, tool or instrument. The 'organismic' (like the 'human relations') approach can be seen partly as an attempt to put men as human beings back into organization. What is relevant here is the imputed relative unimportance of formal structure, managers being permitted great scope to act.[18] Now I see no reason to deny that, on the ground, there will be substantial variation from the crude model I have deduced. I am also prepared to agree that, in appropriate cases, further variations ought to be tried, 'appropriate' being relevant presumably to the technology of the industry. But, knowing something of three large-scale organizations, I do not believe that variation from the *command* model can be so great as to invalidate my thesis. I do not believe that the modern factory system *as a whole* can do without *command*, i.e. without fairly precise differentiation of function and responsibility, hierarchies of authority and technical competence, and fairly elaborate rules of order and procedure, the working out of schedules and other precise time arrangements.[19] Variation there can be but generally only within limits that leave unscathed the idea of a factory as essentially *command.* If so, how congenial will the factory environment prove to the gratification of the workers' needs?

[18] For a discussion, see Tom Burns, *New Society*, 31 Jan. 1963.
[19] Inkeles and Levinson, op. cit., p. 1014.

CHAPTER FOUR

FRUSTRATION 'WITHOUT HOPE'

That, in the absence of countervailing influences, the factory environment will prove extremely uncongenial to the satisfaction of the workers' needs seems an inescapable first approximation. Although we of the comfortable classes too easily allow ourselves to take further comfort from the published figures of average earnings, conveniently overlooking the fate of those whose very low earnings are thereby masked, it will advance the argument to concede that the biogenic needs of the workers are fairly well satisfied in (or, rather, through) the factory of today. Beyond that level, however, needs will *tend* to receive little satisfaction. The need to exercise control over one's working environment, to enjoy a fairly stable, orderly life and foreseeable future, is thwarted at many points. For all the control that the workers *designedly* have (we are still assuming a pre-unionization phase), and for all the knowledge they enjoy of the long-term plans and development of the factory, which may profoundly affect their lives (and their families'), they might as well be chance visitors from outer space. For goal-setting purposes the workers are evidently *in* the factory but not *of* it. The affiliative need tends to be obstructed by the planned impersonality of the factory, where friendly emotions are not among the recommended lubricants. The workers want personal warmth but are expected to be satisfied with organizational coolth. The very terminology is significant: 'hands' (one's face and brain not counting), 'operatives' (extensions of machines), 'personnel' (neutral, grey protoplasm, which, however, reacts to stimuli). The factory structure is meant to be an affectionless structure; that, in a sense, is its strength, but in giving or conferring, it also takes away and denies. As the distribution of esteem generally follows the distribution of authority, only the managers have much of it. Even the possibility of attaining some compensating esteem through the quality of one's work is obstructed by the minute role differentiation, reflecting that minute sub-division of the work from which all sense of making a product in the round has long since been lost. It is doubtful whether, even in Adam Smith's day, anyone could have taken a pride in, or enjoyed a deserved reputation from, making one-eighteenth part of a pin. For making one-eightieth part of a modern product, little esteem is to be expected, either within or without the factory walls; still less from merely assembling the parts. Even if the skill required for each operation were recognized to be greater than is often supposed and if the obvious indispensability of each operation were more readily granted, the attachment of esteem to fragmented work would demand a major effort of the social imagination. Indeed, to give social significance to his own small contribution probably defeats the worker himself as well as the public at large. This must be partly true even where the work is not as finely divided as I have here supposed. On this score too it looks as if only the managers are at all likely to be satisfied.

It follows that in general the workers' self-fulfilling needs—man's highest yearning—never look like being satisfied in the factory. One cannot be one-eightieth creative; and even if the work is rather more than 'semi-skilled', one is still using only a part of one's capacity. Some technical trends such as automation may make some work more rewarding than it now is, but can hardly be expected to be sufficiently offsetting. In any case, the satisfaction of need is obstructed not only by the division of labour in detail but also and perhaps above all by the structure of authority. The business of the command structure is command: to facilitate the setting and re-setting of the goals; the planning and co-ordination of the means of attaining the goals, the verification of the whole co-operative process when it is under way. Even with the most progressive managers, the workers appear on stage only as part of the means. For the business of the manager, as traditionally defined, is to attain the goals of the factory as an organization: i.e. to produce *this* output or render *that* service efficiently, or, if one prefers, *profitably*, so long as the incantation of the term is not allowed to induce self-hypnosis, leading one to believe even now that the extinction of private profit means the extinction of goal-setting and co-ordination by managers, or, therefore, of command by managers. For the satisfaction of their own personal goals, derived from their own root-needs, the workers are left largely to their own devices. Fayol, as we saw, so well understood the problem that he recommended managers to allow subordinates to use their initiative, i.e. to think out and execute a plan, which he rightly characterized as one of the keenest satisfactions for an intelligent man. But he was unable to show how the full play of initiative, especially if conceived as operating all the way down the line, could be reconciled with the requirements of technology and command. For the most part, what the workers are, at present, obliged to accept is at once the most and the least important of the satisfactions they seek: of their biogenic needs. They get, as Maslow observes, bread—but it tends to be bread alone.

All in all, it is tempting to conclude, with the nineteenth-century French social theorist, Fourier, that a factory (in the narrower sense) is 'a mitigated form of convict prison'. The temptation must be resisted, but it is a reasonable expectation (or hypothesis) that a factory in the wider sense is a place where the workers' needs are all too likely to be imprisoned for life. In other words, the probable outcome of the confrontation between workers' needs and factory environment is that the workers will be frustrated. And not simply that. There is reason to think, from experiments and case studies, that the most common response to frustration is a constructive one.[1] In the factory, however, the opportunities for a constructive response seem certain to be few, for the frustrating obstacles can be seen to be the nature of the technology and the authority of management. One must hypothesize, accordingly, that the factory situation is characterized not simply by frustration but, very largely, by frustration 'without hope'.[2] Granted that this

[1] G. W. Allport, J. S. Bruner and E. M. Jandorf, 'Personality Under Social Catastrophe', in C. Kluckhohn, Henry A. Murray and David M. Schneider, *Personality in Nature, Society and Culture*, Knopf, 2nd ed. rev., 1956, ch. 27. Also G. W. Allport, *The Nature of Prejudice*, Doubleday Anchor Book, 1958 ed., ch. 21.

[2] Hilde Himmelweit, 'Frustration and Aggression', in T. H. Pear (ed.), *Psychological Factors of Peace and War*, Hutchinson, 1950, pp. 69–70, quoting F. Alexander. I have followed Himmelweit (pp. 161 and 168) in using 'frustration' in a broad sense to include the case of an external obstacle or blockage, which some writers

hypothesis is plausible, has it the additional merit of being true? Evidently, we must first consider the psychological meaning of frustration 'without hope', the probable responses to it and then see if the expected behaviour can be observed in the factory.

* * * * *

If men are frustrated 'without hope', they suffer an increase of tension, which can be judged by various somatic (or physical) indicators such as the pulse rate, pressure of the blood and hand tremors as well as by observation of their motor activity (roughly, what they do). These physical indicators have certain psychological concomitants: the arousal of strong emotions such as anger and rage, fear and anxiety.[3] The question is: how will this tension be discharged? It will be discharged in various ways, some of which are almost certain, in practice, to be combined; they are treated separately here only for the purpose of analysis.

Aggression (or pugnacity)[4] is *one* common response. It includes not only physical violence but also verbal attack: the lash of the tongue as well as the blow from the strong right arm. Children are the more likely to resort to blows, adults more to violent criticism, swearing and malicious gossip. Adults who, when frustrated, 'do things rather than say things' (as an Oxford City policeman once put it)[5] are liable to end up in court. It was once held that frustration invariably induces aggression and even that aggression always presupposes frustration.[6] The symmetry was pleasing but the theory as a whole failed to carry conviction and was soon modified. It would probably be widely agreed now that 'one-shot prescriptions' (interpreting social difficulties in terms of a single factor

prefer to speak of as 'privation' or 'deprivation', as distinct from an internal conflict giving rise to frustration proper. In this discussion I have drawn mainly on Calvin Hall and Gardner Lindzey, 'Psychoanalytic Theory and Its Application in the Social Sciences', in Gardner Lindzey (ed.), op. cit., vol. I, ch. 4, and their 'Freud's Psychoanalytic Theory', ch. II of Hall and Lindzey (ed.), *Theories of Personality*, Wiley, 1957.

[3] Himmelweit, pp. 169–70.

[4] D. W. Harding, *Social Psychology and Individual Values*, Hutchinson, 1953, p. 21.

[5] *Oxford Times*, 17 July 1964.

[6] J. Dollard, L. W. Doob, N. E. Miller, O. H. Mowrer and R. R. Sears, *Frustration and Aggression*, Yale University Press, 1939.

such as frustration, Oedipus conflict, or economic pressure) will not do.[7] However, one would not doubt that aggression is *a* common response to frustration, even if it had not been induced in a celebrated experiment.[8]

Whether the aggression will be let loose, and on whose luckless head it will fall, depends not only upon the strength of the frustrating experience but also upon various other considerations derived from sociology and the psychology of personality. The sociological factors fall for consideration in the following chapter. As for the other factors, one typology[9] suggests that persons vary not only in their capacity for tolerating frustration, but also in the way in which they distribute the blame for it. Some strike a fair, 'realistic' balance, but some almost automatically blame themselves. Others almost automatically place the blame on other people's shoulders. Thus, other things being equal, those with *extrapunitive* personalities will tend to 'pass on' or *displace* their aggressive feelings. The possible victims range from 'the dog' and 'the wife' to the Jews, Indians, West Indians or Pakistanis, who have it in common that they are often available, 'visible' or conspicuous in some other sense, and are at least rather less likely to retaliate than the frustrating person or obstacle itself.

Such *displacement*, which can be experimentally induced, is unconstructive in that it 'solves nothing', 'finding a scapegoat' being likely to afford only temporary relief. It may even become self-generating.[10] At all events, displacement is conceptually closely related to *projection* and rationalization. Having conveniently re-directed one's aggression to another address, one may take the further step of placing one's *own* anger and hostility at the same door,[11] an operation which has a certain attractive parsimony about it. It is even more parsimonious and neat if one can tack on, by way of explanation and justification, a 'good reason' rather than a 'true one'.[12] This rationalization is

[7] D. O. Hebb and W. R. Thompson, ibid., p. 548.

[8] Cf. Ralph White and Ronald Lippitt in Dorwin Cartwright and Alvin Zander (ed.), *Group Dynamics*, Row, Peterson, 1953, ch. 40.

[9] quoted in Himmelweit, p. 174.

[10] E. F. M. Durbin, and John Bowlby, *Personal Aggressiveness and War*, Kegan Paul, 1939, p. 21.

[11] G. W. Allport, *The Nature of Prejudice*, pp. 236–7, 331, ch. 24 passim.

[12] S. Stansfeld Sargent, *Social Psychology*, The Ronald Press, 1950, p. 178.

another mechanism which has been experimentally-induced, although it perhaps calls for no more support than observation of those about us and rueful inspection of what we ourselves do and say.

According to theory, projection is connected with repression, which is another of the experimentally-observed responses to frustration. In the broad sense, it means the exclusion from awareness of a part or all of a frustrating experience (strictly, of an internal conflict between, roughly, conscience and impulse).[13] It may reveal itself in tenseness, in dreams, lapses of memory or stuttering. In this particular context, repression comes into play so that the memory of a failure to complete a puzzle or solve some problem, and the accompanying frustration, shall be covered over. Repression, however, is never quite complete, and so it is possible for some part of a person's aggressive or destructive impulse, actually 'inside' the man himself, to be projected outwards and to be seen as *emanating from* some other person or persons; it may also be released as a sudden, superficially inexplicable outburst. *Regression* is a possibility: reverting to infantile ways. In the extreme case the grown man acts out the child's role, crawling on the floor and playing with dolls. In the looser sense of a lowering of the level of one's performance, a less mature approach to problems, it has been known, although not invariably, to follow frustration induced in experiments.[14] With regression, one expects *fixation* since regression seems to be *to* a fixated level, i.e., to an earlier stage of psychological growth.[15]

In the cases so far roughly sketched, the frustrated person sticks his ground; theoretically, he might, however, beat a retreat from the scene of his frustration. In the classic phrase of the German-American psychologist, Kurt Lewin, he might

[13] Allport, op. cit., p. 363.

[14] Himmelweit, p. 172. In experiments regression has been equated with a less constructive performance of some task, which is held to indicate a lowering of the mental age level. In this roundabout way regression has some experimental support. R. Barker, T. Dembo and K. Lewin, *Frustration and Regression*, University of Iowa Studies in Child Welfare, 1941, is the classic source.

[15] The experiments on primates and rats cited by Norman R. F. Maier, *Psychology in Industry*, Eng. ed. Harrap, 1946, pp. 65–8, seem to have little to do with fixation in the classical sense. By 'fixation' Maier means a compulsion to do something over and over again even though one knows it will not achieve anything useful. Lady Macbeth's hand-washing, for instance.

go out of the field. This could also perhaps take the form of a psychological retreat into *apathy and resignation*: in experiments as well as case studies of the victims of Nazi persecution and of prolonged unemployment in areas that were Depressed in more senses than one,[16] a flight from real striving and effort to achieve goals was discerned. Such a response presumably implies some fall in the tension requiring immediate relief. At all events, men 'retreated' from (=scaled down) their hopes and expectations; they came to terms with the situation. Another response of this general character is perhaps *fantasy* or *day-dreaming*: one takes refuge from an unpalatable situation in a flight of the imagination, perhaps allowing oneself to be borne aloft by the cheap novelette, women's magazine romance or T.V. high-life serial, but also day-dreaming at work, doing one's job almost automatically.

Obviously, this is an incomplete sketch of a very complicated subject, and acceptable at all only for my limited purpose. That the separation of responses is made only for expository purposes will also bear repetition: in social reality, responses are very likely to be multiple, aggression combining with rationalization, for example. With these qualifications in mind, we may proceed to inquire whether the behaviour that follows from frustration can actually be observed in the factory.

* * * * *

Aggression or pugnacity is so pervasive that it hardly needs documenting. It can be traced in the *undue* criticism of 'the bosses', in malicious gossip and rumour, in swearing and other violent language, in the sabotage of machinery and equipment,[17] in the pretence of mishearing instructions, in playing dumb and in other ways. This whole structure of feeling is, I believe, well caught by G. W. Target in his novel, *The Shop Stewards*.[18] When it comes to the most dramatic form of aggression, the strike, the relevant concept is presumably the number of strikes, corresponding to the number of separate 'centres of frustra-

[16] G. W. Allport, J. S. Bruner, etc., ibid.; Himmelweit, p. 72; E. W. Bakke, *Citizens Without Work*, Yale University Press, 1940.

[17] Maier, op. cit., p. 62.

[18] Duckworth, 1962.

tion'.[19] Here, as opposed to the total number of working days lost (number of strikers × by the numbers of work-days out), the position (at the time of writing) seems to be more serious than at any earlier period in this century. In the generation from 1911 to 1940, there were but five years in which the number of strikes annually exceeded one thousand (1913, 1918–20 and 1937). The peak was reached in 1920, when the total was some 1,600. Since 1941 the total has never been below one thousand. The two thousand-mark was passed in 1944[20] (so much for making strikes illegal). After a falling-off period, the total, from the mid-'fifties, rose steadily towards the three thousand level. Moreover, a much higher proportion of the strikes were unofficial. By contrast, the *general* trend in the number of stoppages in the United States since the war, ignoring some reversal in the early 'fifties, has been downwards, from just under 5,000 in 1946 to some 3,300 in 1963.[21]

It is true that in Britain this trend is, in a sense, the obverse of the decline—and virtual disappearance—of the big stoppage, entailing the loss of many millions of working days. Compared with our experience in the first quarter of this century, the big stoppage itself has been stopped. In the period 1908–14 we lost on average 13 million working days a year; in 1919–25, almost 28 million working days. The average from the beginning of the century to the mid-'fifties was some 10 million working days a year.[22] Early in the 'sixties, our total was of the order of 5 million working days. Compared with the United States, our rate in days lost *per* thousand employees has varied at different times in the post-1945 period from a tenth to rather less than a quarter (in 1963) of theirs.[23] Our stoppages have evidently become short and sharp, bringing out comparatively few men.

It is also true, of course, that the number of strikes varies with the general state of the economy; roughly speaking, the rate falls in depressions and rises when conditions are booming.

[19] Cf. K. G. J. C. Knowles, *Strikes—A Study in Industrial Conflict*, Blackwell, 1954, p. 145, where the number of strikes is taken to indicate the prevalence of 'separate outbreaks of discontent'.

[20] ibid., statistical appendix, table IV.

[21] United States Information Service, *Labour News from the U.S.*, Sept. 1964.

[22] H. A. Clegg, 'Strikes', *Political Quarterly*, XXVII, Jan.–March 1956.

[23] ibid.; *International Labour Review*, July 1955; *Labour News from the United States*, Sept. 1964.

In the 1930s, for instance, the number of strikes was of the order of 300–400 a year. But, as usual, such a statistical correlation explains nothing in itself; it merely invites inquiry. Its psychological meaning would seem to be partly that in boom conditions aggression can be prudently given rein, but that in depressions it is generally inhibited.

For, of course, the tendency to aggression cannot always be given its head. Himmelweit's evidence suggests that it will be checked by a fear of punishment, by a feeling of insecurity and by great differences in status between those who evoke the frustration and those who experience it.[24] In periods of depression the workers' feeling of insecurity is obviously intense, and their fear of punishment at the hands of those with high status and authority (the managers) is correspondingly acute. In such conditions one would expect the workers *generally* to inhibit their aggression, and this seems to be what happens, judging by the number of strikes. Of course, some groups of workers may be unable to contain themselves, for the strength of aggression depends not only on 'the situation' but also on the strength of the frustrating experience. So a pattern in which a comparatively small number of strikes is shot through with a few large stoppages involving a vast loss in working days is entirely comprehensible. If we could assume that frustration in the coal mining and textiles industries was peculiarly strong in about the first three decades of this century, that might well (with the general state of the economy) explain much of the pattern of the period, for it was the big stoppages in these fields that largely accounted for the now almost unbelievable totals of working days lost.

These are only tentative remarks in a most complex subject; I should like to be judged not on a single paragraph but on the argument as a whole. If I am right, then in a period of depression or of economic chaos (such as the runaway inflation in Germany in the 1920s), the displacement of aggression (other mechanisms held constant) ought to be high. It has often been suggested, for example, that the Jews were the tragic victims of the German people's displacement-aggression. Whether this was so, I am in no position to judge. I must be content to resume the main line of this section of the chapter, i.e. to

[24] Himmelweit, op. cit., p. 177.

continue to inquire whether the behaviour expected to follow from frustration can actually be observed in the factory. If the command structure of the factory and conditions outside it inhibit or limit aggression, one expects aggression to be displaced. A hint that this process does occur may be taken from the fact that workers dissatisfied with their jobs are far more likely to be anti-Semitic than those who express satisfaction,[25] which suggests that here again the Jews were involuntarily discharging their historic role as scapegoats. Similarly, the resentful steel worker, tired of the heat and the noise and finding the world out of joint because of his failure to qualify as an engineer, rails against 'the Goddam Jews who run this place'. This was in a factory where neither the management nor ownership was Jewish.[26] But unco-operativeness towards fellow-workers on the job, mutual disparagement, sending a man to Coventry and similar actions suggest, in some instances, modes of displacement; even a machine or the final product[27] may be a hapless victim.

Direct evidence (a hint even) of that process of projection which is to be anticipated with displacement is not, so far as I know, available for the industrial scene. One can only speculate whether the hostility that the men ascribe to 'the bosses' and 'the capitalists' does not represent, in part, their own emotions 'reflected back'. I do not claim that everything is reflection. No doubt, what management 'feels about' the workers is autonomous; its perspective is so different and the tendency of the present industrial arrangements to create a certain sort of worker-personality is so marked, that their attitudes must have comparatively objective roots. But it may be that part of what the workers see as coming from management is what they themselves have sent out in the first place. If so, it represents a peculiar and hard-to-break circular flow of emotions. Rationalization, on the other hand, does seem to be accounted for. Some of the justifications for 'whipping' tools and materials from one's employer are almost text-book examples of rationalization. 'The employers exploit us, so why shouldn't we get a bit of our own back?' 'We are robbed

[25] G. W. Allport, *The Nature of Prejudice*, p. 331, citing A. A. Campbell.
[26] ibid., p. 330.
[27] J. A. C. Brown (who has had experience of industry), op. cit., pp. 230–1.

all the time, therefore we are justified in robbing'. 'It isn't poor people who will lose by it.'[28]

Like projection, repression is by its very nature difficult to trace in the factory. Yet it represents the most plausible interpretation of the sillier sort of strike—over something trivial or even quite untenable. Even allowing for inadequate and biased reporting, such strikes surely do occur. They may well be accounted for, at least in part, by aggression which, repressed over a period, is now triggered off by some incident or action that may be serious in itself, although still disproportionate to the 'blow up', or perhaps utterly trivial. Some unofficial 'walk-outs' and other behaviour of the kind might well originate in that way.

The most obvious, indeed literal, sense of 'going out of the field' is to leave the job altogether. For at least thirty years or so now the rate of labour turnover has been taken as one probable index of social unrest (though not to the exclusion of other explanations). It was observed in the United States that the unskilled worker had a much higher turnover than the skilled worker.[29] Even some well-paid skilled workers in some factories had a high rate of turnover that could not be attributed to rational economic calculation; these workers, in fact, just drifted around and even back to where they started from. The interpretation offered was that most of the turnover represented 'emotional unrest', derived from poverty in social work relationship.[30] This seems to be tantamount to saying that the labour turnover was largely due to frustration on the job. A more specific link between labour turnover (and voluntary absenteeism) and frustration has since been established in investigations at an American manufacturer's plant.[31]

[28] Knowles, op. cit., p. 210, n. 1, citing John Hilton, a former professor of industrial relations at Cambridge. My conversations with shop stewards suggest that the practice is widespread. In December, 1965, a man was charged at Oxford with stealing a tool kit and an engine unit worth almost £300 ($840) from the Morris Motors' factory, Cowley, which the defending solicitor (lawyer) described as 'a thieves' kitchen, where you could persuade someone to get you anything'. *Oxford Times*, 31 Dec. 1965.

[29] S. Howard Patterson, *Social Aspects of Industry*, McGraw-Hill, 1935, cited in T. N. Whitehead, *Leadership in a Free Society*, Oxford University Press, 1936, p. 17.

[30] Whitehead, ibid.

[31] Lester Coch and John R. P. French, Jr., 'Overcoming Resistance to Change' in Dorwin Cartwright and Alvin Zander, op. cit., p. 261.

Even where workers remain wedded to a particular factory, much of their behaviour is consistent with the idea of 'going out of the field' psychologically. Voluntary absenteeism may be partly explained in that way. In coal mining, for instance, the absentees in 1964 were so numerous on Fridays and Mondays that many collieries were operating with only three-quarters or even half of the labour force.[32] No doubt the miners do suffer from the disadvantage of being so much measured;[33] even so, their behaviour now, long after nationalization, is a reminder of the frustration already tentatively diagnosed in terms of the big stoppages that once characterized their industry. There is some more specific evidence, too, of the relationship between absenteeism and frustration from the Durham coal-field; there the high absenteeism of the filler (who shovels shot coal on to the conveyor) and of the stoneman (who works in the 'gateway', shovelling shot coal, erecting supports, etc.) seems to have been a function of frustration.[34]

Some accidents, too, seem to demand interpretation as a 'going out of the field'. In two Scottish adjoining collieries where men from the same village worked on the same seam, the accident rate in one was three times that of the other. The difference was attributed to differences in morale, which may perhaps be loosely equated with frustration. In a particular R.A.F. squadron the number of crashes increased with the increase in their collective frustration, and was reduced when the frustration was reduced.[35] In such cases as these, men might be said to be opting out, unconsciously, of a frustrating situation. This may also apply to some industrial illness. Industrial dermatitis may arise from some 'genuine' irritant but a high incidence has occurred after handling such innocuous substances such as soap, cosmetics and cold cream. When that happens a connection with morale and general discontent has 'invariably' been detected. Since another industrial dermatologist has characterized the disease as 95% emotional,[36] we are

[32] *The Guardian*, 10 July 1964, reporting the chairman of the National Coal Board.

[33] H. A. Turner, *The Trend of Strikes*, Leeds University Press, p. 6.

[34] E. L. Trist, G. W. Higgin, H. Murray and A. B. Pollock, *Organizational Choice*, Tavistock Publications, 1963, pp. 56 and 61.

[35] J. A. C. Brown, op. cit., p. 259, citing T. T. Paterson, pp. 263–4.

[36] ibid., citing two dermatologists, Dr. J. H. Twiston Davies and Dr. Mark Hewitt.

the more inclined to suspect that frustration is at work here again.

Accident neuroses, too, may be grist to our mill. It is said to be the rule that industrial accidents (such as an injury to the head) are followed by neurotic complications, whereas in sport and hunting such a sequel is almost unknown. One possible explanation of the difference is that the industrial situation harbours resentment, which might be loosely identified with frustration. In general, the higher the morale, the fewer the accident neuroses.[37] All this is very far from being conclusive, but, in the context of the many other covert instances of 'going out of the field', it is at least suggestive of the forces at work.

Of the other possible forms of withdrawal, apathy in industry is surely a matter of common knowledge. Senior supervisors and foremen often remark upon it, citing the unwillingness of the rank and file to accept promotion. Apathy has been observed, too, in Swedish workers, and in those American motor car workers who, having lost hope of bettering themselves, have finally abandoned 'the American dream'.[38] Regression may here work hand in hand with apathy and resignation, workers becoming less constructive or mature in the sense of doing only just enough work to 'get by' and no more. Irresponsible behaviour, loss of emotional control, uncritical responsiveness to rumours, unreasoning fears, horse-play and the formation of childish cliques have also been interpreted by an industrial psychologist in terms of regression.[39] Blind resistance to change might perhaps be a sign of the closely related mechanism of fixation; so too with the inability to tackle new problems and situations effectively. In this instance behaviour seems 'frozen', and the new, required responses are prevented or delayed. For withdrawal into a wish-fulfilling world while still in the factory, the evidence is much firmer. Much of it comes from the reports of our own Industrial Fatigue Research Board; before the war, day-dreaming at work was found to be widespread.[40] The fantasies provide a magic-carpet flight from unsatisfying work.

* * * * *

[37] ibid., p. 265.

[38] Ely Chinoy, *Automobile Workers and the American Dream*, Random House, 1955.

[39] Maier, op. cit., p. 64.

[40] Argyris, p. 89, citing S. Wyatt and others.

So far, so good; or at least, not so bad. Much of the anticipated behaviour does seem to be displayed, and to that extent we are encouraged. But against the grain of the argument it must be asked: cannot the observed behaviour be explained in other ways? Even if the behaviour *does* derive from frustration, can one show that the frustration is derived from the structure of command? Is there any other behaviour, including verbal behaviour (what workers say) that seems to contradict the thesis? Only the second of these questions has been given its due by the leading writers in this genre. Yet not one of the three can be shirked.

It has already been conceded (at the end of chapter Two) that the young recruits to the factory will arrive with their characters partly formed. Thus some part of the behaviour observed in the factory will have been 'imported' as a series of tendencies or propensities; for example, in the Freudian mode, a tendency to aggression. Alternatively, or in addition, we can say, on the model of chimpanzees, that some hostility is currently derived from fear.[41] And of course some hostility has a comparatively 'rational' source in a dispute about the share of the product going to profits and interest as opposed to wages and salaries. In some strikes no doubt the black hand of agitators may be discerned. So, too, with some other examples of observed behaviour. A high labour turnover may be due to market forces or (pre-war) to a bullying foreman. Both high turnover and voluntary absenteeism may be partly due to objectively bad working conditions. This holds good for some accidents too (e.g. bad lighting or badly-placed machines), with fatigue or accident proneness contributing. The workers may have been apathetic before they were signed on. So the qualifications might continue.

Accordingly, it has to be admitted that some part of the observed behaviour may have sources other than frustration: the proportions are a matter for research. Yet we must not exaggerate. Trained observers of the industrial scene, such as industrial psychologists, do observe and emphasize frustration in the factory.[42] Insofar as agitators do stir up strikes, some may

[41] Hebb and Thompson, ibid., pp. 548–52.

[42] Maier, esp. ch. 4; Brown, ch. 9, esp. p. 255; David Krech and Richard C. Crutchfield, *Theory and Problems of Social Psychology*, McGraw-Hill, 1948, p. 553; Knowles, pp. 214–18.

have to be seen rather as catalytic agents than as first causes, releasing repressed aggression arising from frustration in the factory: this might be the significance of the blowing of whistles ('all out'). If we try to explain accidents in alternative ways, e.g. objectively bad working conditions, we are not uncommonly left with the puzzle of variations in the rate when conditions are identical. Some such factor as morale—which is bound up with frustration—has then to be introduced into the equation in order to account for the facts.

Perhaps above all, if the various forms of behaviour were for the most part responses to frustration and if responses are likely in practice to be mixed up, then the presumed responses ought to show a sort of family connection. This they do show. A generation ago in the United States a study concluded that labour turnover was as important a sign of industrial unrest as strikes and other industrial conflict.[43] For this country, Knowles, author of the standard book on British strikes, provides evidence for the view that strikes and voluntary absenteeism are 'interchangeable' forms of unrest. Another British student, R. W. Revans, found 'plenty of evidence', not only in collieries but also in groups of factories (in the usual sense), that absence through sickness goes hand in hand with absence from other causes: in some instances, the accident rate is linked with the rate of voluntary absenteeism; in others, it is linked with the strike rate. The psychologist J. A. C. Brown reports a strong positive correlation between accident-proneness and voluntary absenteeism.[44] As these are exactly the types of interconnections that the theory leads us to expect, it seems to me that the onus is on those who discount this kind of approach[45] to provide a better theory to account for these patterns of industrial behaviour. The most parsimonious theory so far adduced does seem to be the theory of frustration, although no one pretends that it explains everything. On balance, I think it reasonable to conclude that the observed behaviour does substantially derive from current frustration in the factory.

* * * * *

[43] cited in T. N. Whitehead, p. 17.

[44] Knowles, pp. 225–6; R. W. Revans, 'Industrial Morale and the Size of Unit', *Political Quarterly*, Vol. XXVII, no. 3, 1956, pp. 304–11; Brown, p. 258.

[45] H. A. Turner, ibid.

Granted that the frustration is present, does it come substantially from where the theory says it does? Delbert Miller and William Form, authors of a well-known American text on industrial sociology, see dissatisfaction in American industry rather in terms of the socialization of young Americans and so of the expectations and aspirations that they bring to the factory. When American workers fail to get at work the satisfaction, including the personal recognition, that they have been led to expect, they do experience frustration and anxiety.[46] That allowance must be made for pre-factory socialization has already been agreed. All the same I think that here at least the significance of command-induced frustration still remains. We may take a bearing on the subject by bringing into focus the causes of strikes as the principal overt form of aggression. The difficulty immediately encountered is that the Ministry of Labour statistics are not only made to fit into amateurish categories apparently acquired in a fit of abstraction over half a century ago and hardly changed since, but that these statistics pass off as causes what the participants chose to *say about* the causes at the time of the dispute. Since so much motivation is unconscious, the participants cannot be expected to be enlightening about causes.[47] If, however, the statistics are taken at their face value, we find that fewer than half the stoppages, involving rather more than six out of ten of the total of workers directly affected, are 'caused by' wage disputes in their various forms, including, for convenience, disputes about the hours of labour. About the same proportion of strikes, involving more than a quarter of the total number of workers directly affected, largely derives from the command structure of the workshop: the reinstatement of workers; objections to foremen and other supervisors; promotion or re-engagement after redundancy; managerial refusals to negotiate with a trade union, and the like.[48] Even in a period (1927–47) embracing very different

[46] Delbert C. Miller and William H. Form, *Industrial Sociology*, Harper and Row, 2nd ed., 1964, pp. 618–19.

[47] Arthur Kornhauser, 'Human Motivation Underlying Industrial Conflict', in Arthur Kornhauser, Robert Dubin and Arthur M. Ross, *Industrial Conflict*, McGraw-Hill, 1954, p. 64.

[48] William McCarthy, 'The Reasons Given for Striking', *Bulletin* 21, of the Oxford University Institute of Statistics, Blackwell, 1959, Table I, and pp. 23–5 and 27.

economic conditions, the command structure may have been the source of three or four out of every ten strikes.[49] For the modern period a Trades Union Congress survey seems to lend support: it found that barely one third (32%) of the strikes in 1958–59 concerned wages and bonus payments; almost as many (29%) were rooted in dismissals—of shop stewards or of other members on disciplinary grounds (20%), or in the form of redundancy (9%).[50] If one adds another 12% for strikes arising from recognition issues and the alleged breaking of agreements by management, then the 'command' proportion grows.

Interpretation as distinct from bare statistics seems to point in the same direction. What is shown as a strike about wages may well be traceable to some other source. Although the converse is also possible, it is significant that the author of the standard work on British strikes considers that, in the period 1911–45, the number of strikes officially attributed to wages issues exaggerated 'the strictly monetary motives'.[51] The strikes so recorded were often symbols of other dissatisfactions. On the other hand, the 'command' element appears to have been under-estimated. William McCarthy, analysing the period 1945–57, concluded that eight strikes out of ten (involving seven out of ten of the total directly affected) were attributable to changes in the system of wage payment, to changes in 'other working arrangements, rules and discipline', and to alleged attacks on the customs and practices of the trade.[52] As he also judged that some of the strikes over wage payment were really indirect attacks by management on restrictive practices and 'featherbedding', it does seem that much of this overt form of aggression can be traced, via frustration, to the command structure of the factory.

It seems probable, too, that some aggression in its various covert forms (pretending not to hear instructions; rule-breaking 'by mistake'; leaving the job before time, and the like) can be

[49] Knowles, p. 234.

[50] T.U.C., *Report on Disputes and Workshop Representation*, Sept. 1960.

[51] Knowles, p. 219. Cf. Kornhauser, ibid., on wage demands as 'unverbalized strivings for self-respect and dignity or vague hostilities towards the boss, the machine, and the entire industrial discipline'.

[52] McCarthy, pp. 27–8.

traced back to autocratic leadership in the factory,[53] i.e. to the element of command. It is even possible that accident-proneness may be in part an attribute of men 'resentful of authority', accident-prone men not being clumsy or dull but quick-witted men of action.[54] One must, of course, admit that some of the observable behaviour derives, via frustration, from sources other than the structure of authority. The most obvious of these is without doubt that basic and closely related feature, the division of labour in detail, from which the differential rate of turnover between skilled and unskilled workers in the U.S.A.,[55] voluntary absenteeism in the Durham coalfield,[56] apathy and resignation in Swedish industry[57] appear in part to derive. Without further research no one can be certain of the relative importance of these two factors as sources of frustration. All the same, the structure of command does seem very likely to be the more, even the most, substantial single source. For, apart from anything so far discussed, it is precisely that element in industry that has been challenged, in varying degrees, by every scheme of industrial reform from co-partnership through Guild Socialism to workers' control.[58] That being so, the argument can, I think, be allowed to proceed.

* * * * *

We still have to jump one more obstacle, however, before we reach the home straight. What men *do* in the factory is consistent with the theory of frustration, but *some* part of what they *say* appears to be inconsistent. In a 1947 survey covering 3,000 engineering workers in the Birmingham area (a random sample of 30,000), almost six out of ten declared that they liked their job. Fewer than two out of ten said that they disliked it or were bored by it. Out of every ten men in two mass-production factories and six metal-rolling mills, six or seven

[53] Brown, pp. 230–1 and 235–6. He does not himself make this connection specifically but that is the context and drift of the discussion from p. 225 onwards.

[54] ibid., p. 258.

[55] See Arthur W. Kornhauser in Bernard Berelson and Morris Janowitz, *Reader in Public Opinion and Communication*, The Free Press, 1950, p. 71, n. 1 for post-World War I evidence in U.S.A.; for later periods see Whitehead, p. 17 and Argyris, p. 81.

[56] See above n. 34.

[57] Argyris, p. 91.

[58] See below, Part II.

declared themselves 'satisfied' or 'very satisfied' with the operations they performed. Evidence from the Netherlands and from the United States, where the study of job satisfaction has been a minor industry in itself, can be cited in support. Thus many American surveys, pre-war and post-war, national samples as well as local samples covering various occupations, suggest that eight out of ten are satisfied.[59]

Yet one can hardly leap from such findings to the conclusion that 'every' survey of workers' attitudes, no matter what industry, indicates that 'most workers like their job'.[60] The evidence, in fact, is conflicting. A 1947 *Fortune* poll disclosed that the proportion of factory workers who said that their job was interesting was little more than half. In the following year, when *Fortune* put the same question to young men aged 18–25, only some four out of ten factory workers (in the narrow sense) and barely six out of ten non-factory manual workers said they were satisfied.[61] A decade earlier, a survey of young Americans working in canning factories and textile mills disclosed that very nearly all of them did not simply dislike the job but hated it.[62]

One of the difficulties in such surveys is evidently the avoidance of ambiguity. For instance, in one survey the question put was: 'taking into consideration all the things about your job (work), how satisfied or dissatisfied are you with it?'[63] This fails to distinguish between intrinsic job satisfaction and 'overall liking for the job situation',[64] which I take to mean those social satisfactions *on* the job such as might account for the return of the three British football-pools winners to their rather humdrum work.[65] Industrial psychologists who have closely examined surveys of job satisfaction have also pointed out the 'dangerous inadequacy' of summary statements of the type: '80% of the workers interviewed expressed general

[59] Brown, p. 191; Morris Viteles, *Motivation and Morale in Industry*, Staples Press, 1954, pp. 9–10; R. Blauner in W. Galenson and S. M. Lipset, *Labour and Trade Unionism*, Wiley, 1960, pp. 340–1.

[60] Brown, p. 190.

[61] Blauner, pp. 342 and 356, n. 12.

[62] Daniel Katz in Arthur Kornhauser, Robert Dubin and Arthur M. Ross (ed.), op. cit., p. 91.

[63] Blauner, p. 341.

[64] Katz, p. 91.

[65] Brown, pp. 188 and 190.

satisfaction with their jobs'.[66] Feelings of satisfaction or dissatisfaction are complex not simple. One may be satisfied with many of the conditions of one's work but distinctly dissatisfied with other conditions; the proportion recorded as 'dissatisfied' will depend upon an arbitrary definition in the particular case. Above all, workers may not want or be able to answer such questions with complete honesty. There is, indeed, a 'certain naivety in expecting frank and simple answers to job questions in a society where one's work is so important a part of one's self that to demean one's job is to question one's own competence'.[67] To say that one is dissatisfied is to court the risk of defining oneself as a failure. Another possible interpretation is that an answer of 'satisfied' merely means that one has 'taken into consideration' *everything*; i.e. that having made a realistic appraisal of one's life-chances, especially as determined by one's education, one has lowered one's aspirations, and is jogging along, making the best of it. One is 'satisfied' because one has 'scaled down' sharply, come to terms with one's fate. One American survey does support this interpretation. In that, over eight out of ten said they were satisfied, but fewer than three out of ten thought that they had a very good or even a fairly good chance of getting on.[68] It is also worth bearing in mind the substantial proportion who would choose another career if they had their time over again: four out of ten even among skilled men in steel-making and car production in the United States, and just over half among printers.[69]

Besides, there is the hard evidence of what men actually do in the factory as distinct from what they say. What they do would be inexplicable if they were as truly satisfied as some of their answers indicate. Strike action is only a part of what they do, but H. A. Clegg's interpretation of it in terms of 'spiritual grievances'—railing against the world, the boss, their fate—is extremely suggestive.[70] For on the basis of frustration theory, a general acceptance of one's fate (being 'satisfied', *all things considered*) is quite compatible with sporadic 'lashings-out'

[66] Arthur Kornhauser quoted by Blauner, p. 353, n. 7.
[67] ibid.
[68] Survey Research Centre, Michigan, cited in Argyris, p. 93.
[69] Blauner, pp. 342–3.
[70] ibid., p. 42.

against it. Indeed the mechanism of repression alone requires one to look out for exactly such a pattern of behaviour.

For all these reasons, I do not think that those surveys of job satisfaction that seem to tell a different tale, while they cannot with propriety be ignored, are at all fatal to the argument. Thus two tentative conclusions seem permissible. Although some of the behaviour observable in the factory may have been imported 'in' the partly-formed characters of the young workers, or currently induced in some other conceivable ways, much of it, despite some workers' remarks to the contrary, does stem from current frustration. Secondly, the greater part *of* that frustration appears to have the command structure of the factory as its source. Even allowing in special cases for some modifications along 'organismic' lines, it looks (at this stage of the argument) as if one's first impression is the correct one—that the factory environment will indeed be extremely uncongenial to the satisfaction of the workers' root-needs. For, since *command* is inherent in all factories, the tendency is not simply towards frustration but towards frustration 'without hope'.

CHAPTER FIVE

PRIMARY GROUPS IN THE FACTORY

In the factory, then, the workers find barriers across their path. If, however, their needs are really as fundamental as we have so far supposed, we should expect them to try, if only half-consciously, to achieve gratification in other ways. That they do so partly in their leisure hours, as for instance in various social activities and in hobbies, is evident. Such 'dissociation' has even been advocated for the worker on the analogy of the peacetime conscript and his unsatisfying military life.[1] But even if 'dissociation' were to be in a high degree attainable, it would not redound to the advantage of good industrial relations, for the factory would then come to be perceived more than ever as a place where gratification of one's needs is to be expected chiefly after leaving it. It is doubtful, in any case, how far 'dissociation' is at present psychologically possible. The workers still spend five days a week inside the walls, and, even without the systematic overtime that is so common, each day extends over about eight hours. The former general secretary of the T.U.C., Lord Citrine, from his exceptionally long and wide experience of industry, is surely a wiser guide:

> 'I can tell you this: you'll always get poor industrial relations where workers do not feel that as well as earning their bread in a factory they are somehow *living* as well, growing in their work, developing their characters, their minds.'[2]

Again, a man's job virtually defines him. 'What does he *do*?' we whisper of the man whose name we managed to catch but not his occupation. For these reasons at least, we must be prepared for a kind of countervailing tendency or effort inside the factory.

[1] Quoted in Knowles, p. 216.

[2] Lord Citrine, former general secretary of the T.U.C., in an interview with Kenneth Harris of the *Observer*, 17 Sept. 1961.

Such an effort crystallizes, where technology permits, in the formation of primary groups within the factory. By *primary group*, its inventor, the American sociologist, C. H. Cooley meant a social group 'characterized by intimate face-to-face association and co-operation', such as a family or circle of friends. How far the attribute of being face-to-face is crucial to the concept of a primary group, and whether such groups are as resistant to the pressure of events and processes (e.g. industrialism) as Cooley seemed to imply, need not detain us here.[3] What is more to the point is whether the concept applies to groups in factories. In his study of three substantial plants in the American Mid-West in the 1950s, the psychologist Robert Dubin concluded that work was not a 'central life interest' of industrial man, and, in particular, that barely 10% of the men in those plants perceived their important primary relations as subsisting there. For such relations the rest looked outside the plant.[4] How far these findings hold good generally is a matter for further research. Meanwhile, it is not inconvenient to make do in an industrial context with a somewhat weaker sense of *primary group* than obtains when discussing the family. Cooley can provide quite well for that weaker sense. He allows not only for self-assertion and some friction in primary groups, which in industry would be of more than common significance, but also for a 'we-feeling' as their identifying feature. Working groups enjoying such a sense of identity are surely common in industry even if they fall short of real intimacy.

Such primary groups are common because they represent virtual (i.e., not altogether conscious) attempts on the part of workers to gratify root-needs that tend to be obstructed in the ways already roughly sketched. Evidently primary groups serve some of the workers' biogenic needs. Hanging together, the workers (like Cabinet Ministers) at least avoid hanging separately, and no doubt achieve positive gains, as, for instance, in bargaining about wages (taken as a means of satisfying

[3] *Social Organization*, Scribner, 1929 (first ed. 1909), p. 23; Ellsworth Faris, *American Journal of Sociology*, vol. 38, 1932, pp. 41–50. See also George Homans, *The Human Group*, Harcourt, Brace, 1950.

[4] Robert Dubin, in Arnold M. Rose, *Human Behaviour and Social Processes*, Routledge and Kegan Paul, 1962, ch. 13. Cf. Robert Blauner, *Alienation and Freedom*, University of Chicago Press, 1964, p. 183.

some biogenic needs). In more familiar language, the primary group serves an economic purpose.

This is so obvious that historically it obscured the other functions of the primary group. It was not until restriction of output began to be studied academically a generation ago that the controlling power and other functions of the primary work-group came very gradually to be understood. In a study of unorganized (i.e. non-union) workers in the U.S.A., Mathewson discovered that restriction of output was widespread: in 105 establishments embracing 39 industries.[5] Now there were (in the workers' eyes) compelling economic reasons for informal-group arrangements to restrict output: to avoid working oneself out of a job or a cut in the rates. All the same the researcher judged that these justifications were in part rationalizations, and that restriction had much more to do with maintaining the solidarity of the group than with economic calculation. In the language of this discussion, the primary work-group was being put at the service not only of biogenic needs but also of the need for safety or control.

This was also the main impression that the world gained from the researches of the Harvard teams conducted at 'Hawthorne' between 1927 and 1932 and published by various hands in the three years before the war. It was from those researches at the Hawthorne (near Chicago) factory of the Western Electric Company that one learned to see the non-economic purposes of the primary group. It was never true that these investigators denied the economic functions: discussing restriction of output, which was the particular group norm that was stumbled upon and stressed, Whitehead remarked in 1936 that the men feared a cut in piece-rates if output exceeded the level they had informally set.[6] Yet it is true that the Hawthorne researchers, under the influence of the Italian sociologist, Vilfredo Pareto's teaching about the 'non-logical' roots of behaviour, did stress the 'non-logical' (or, roughly, non-economic) element in restrictive practices. For example, one

[5] Stanley B. Mathewson, *Restriction of Output Among Unorganized Workers*, Viking Press, 1931, quoted in T. N. Whitehead, *Leadership in a Free Society*, Oxford University Press, 1936, p. 18.

[6] Whitehead, pp. 18 and 57; F. J. Roethlisberger and W. J. Dickson, *Management and the Worker*, Harvard University Press, 1939.

of their later (1931–32) experiments at Hawthorne involved a group of fourteen men, most of whom were employed in attaching insulated wire to banks of electrical terminals. Under the eyes of a supervisor (and a social scientist), these wiremen worked in three sub-groups of three, each sub-group having the services of a man to solder the connections. Two inspectors scrutinized the completed units. Despite a piecework incentive scheme, the workers deliberately restricted output to a level they considered appropriate, and put pressure on potential deviants to keep them in line. In other words, the standard informally reached became a group norm reinforced by sanctions. Thus the group achieved a form of control over current operations that was also a kind of insurance against an unpredictable future. In large part, the group was really attempting to avert the danger of change,[7] or at least to 'manage' change. In short, the primary group was serving the workers' need for safety rather than their biogenic needs.

In recent years the pendulum has swung the other way, bringing about a more 'logical' interpretation of restrictive practices by primary work-groups. Donald Roy, the American who as worker-sociologist spent almost a year as a drill press operator, showing a devotion to his sociological craft worthy of a worker-priest to his religious faith, reports many a vivid conversation-piece embodying a very cool calculation of the workers' economic interests. New recruits to the working group were first taught how to go slow under the very eyes of the rate-setter, so that a comfortable or even a slow time might be obtained for a quick job. Once the new recruit became skilful, he was taught to keep production at such a level as would not endanger the rate that had been set.[8] For this country, R. P. Lynton, the wartime engineering operative turned peacetime manager, has drawn a similar picture: the older mentor of the young worker, teaching him how much could be 'safely' produced; informal group agreements to take twice as long over a piece of work as it at first demanded; the spun-out time; the hiding of the 'surplus' finished products. More recently, Lupton, a leading English industrial sociologist, has attributed

[7] Whitehead, p. 57.

[8] William F. Whyte, *Money and Motivation*, Harper, 1955, Part I.

an economic purpose (quite plainly, 'a fiddle') to the restrictive practices he observed.[9]

Thus the emphasis has changed. Yet the lesson we can draw from 'Hawthorne' is still of immense significance: the primary work-group does serve workers' needs other than the biogenic. It does serve their safety need, for instance, and not merely by restrictive practices: it affords protection for the individual worker in quite another sense. Although the process has been little documented, the primary group in effect loosens the strait jacket in which the individual is placed by the factory organization. Seeing a worker in the round, accepting his quirks and shibboleths, the primary group in effect takes the formal rules and procedures and bends them to meet individual cases. It puts, in short, a protective shield around its individual members.

Turning to the affiliative need, we see that another 'Hawthorne' insight remains of great importance. In the factory as designed, the workers are cogs, and rightly so *once* we grant that the achievement of the factory's objectives, as distinct from the satisfaction of individual needs, is paramount. Whatever the defectiveness of the relay assembly test room experiment (the 1927–32 'Hawthorne' research), it is plain that the girls, set apart from the others, developed a comparatively full social life, off as well as on the job. Common experience and uncommon research support the remark that workers are unlikely to put up indefinitely with an impoverished social present. If the current activity is continuous [unlike a peacetime conscript's], and if its social context is insufficiently rich, great efforts will be made to supply the deficiency.[10] That is to say, the worker will seek to gratify his or her affiliative need, in part, in a primary work-group. In it he ceases to be simply a worker and becomes a person, with a name as distinct from a number on a card, an identity, where in some degree he is valued for himself. His uniqueness begins to peep through the undifferentiated lumps of mere labour. Relations in the group will no doubt be less warm and intense than relations in the family,

[9] *Incentives and Management in British Industry*, Routledge and Kegan Paul, 1949; T. Lupton, *On the Shop Floor*, Pergamon Press, Oxford, 1963.

[10] Whitehead, pp. 22–3; A. Zaleznik, *Worker Satisfaction and Development*, Harvard University, Graduate School of Business Administration, 1956, p. 78.

but may yet be significant for industrial relations. For if this alternative way of partly gratifying the affiliative root-need suffers obstruction, unrest may well follow, which will not be removed simply by paying higher wages, for that merely satisfies some of the biogenic needs, whereas what is required is an enrichment of present social living, some gratifying of the need to 'belong'.

How far primary groups in the factory meet the workers' need for esteem (or recognition) is very difficult to judge, so meagre is our information. It is probable, however, that in their primary group workers receive *some* gratification not only of their affiliative need but also of their need for esteem: they win some respect as well as affection. If so, then once again the factory organization, with the distribution of esteem more or less following the line of authority, is subject to some informal modification or revision.

Up to this point, then, it seems likely that the primary group in the factory generally contributes to the gratification of the workers' needs, although not necessarily at any particular point in time, since immediate gratification (e.g. of some biogenic needs via wages) may have to be sacrificed on occasion in the interests, say, of group solidarity. (Here the needs approach begins to reveal its complexity). On the other hand, at the very highest level of root-need, it appears that the primary group hinders rather than helps. Here again we are inadequately briefed, but there is reason to fear that the primary group seals off workers from the possibility of self-fulfilment at work. For 'natural' as the primary group undoubtedly is, its ethos is not creative. Its gift lies in self-defence, not advance; where self-fulfilment requires growth, it demands restriction. More, it may even demand destruction. Deliberately damaging one's tools (e.g. breaking a drill)[11] in order to bluff a higher rate for the job, and deliberately wasting time after the job has been set and agreed, is disabling enough: to hide away or wantonly destroy even one part of what has just been turned out is a calamity. In destroying worked-up material, the worker is in some degree destroying himself.

On balance, it seems, judging almost as much from the tone and temper of the various research reports and discussions as

[11] Whyte, p. 17.

from their substantive conclusions, that the primary group in effect lifts workers to somewhere about the middle level of their needs-hierarchy. That is, it helps the gratification of some of the biogenic needs as well as part of the safety and affiliative needs and, possibly, the need for esteem. Thereafter it brings no relief. (In the alternative formulation,[12] dispensing with the notion of hierarchy, one could simply say that the primary group serves some of the biogenic needs—via bargaining—as well as the power and affiliative needs but hardly the need for achievement.)

* * * * *

If that assessment is fairly near the mark, what effect will the emergence of primary groups have on the general situation in the factory? The answer depends upon the nice balancing of a number of factors. Insofar as the primary group affords an alternative mode of satisfying, in part, some of the workers' needs, then (other things remaining unchanged) that level of frustration which the factory structure, unimpeded, would tend to induce must be kept lower than it would otherwise have been. Even the residual frustration may be a little more easily borne, since a friendly setting is thought to minimize (*not* eliminate) the effects of a frustrating experience.[13] Thus the various behavioural consequences of frustration ought to be less serious than they would have been had no primary group been formed. Even positive gains are conceivable. By, in effect, treating workers as persons, for instance, the primary group may evoke efforts and loyalties that were previously only dormant.[14] All in all, the primary work-group might well seem to be 'functional' for the factory, i.e., roughly, tending to facilitate the achievement of its objectives (say, a certain output at a certain cost or price).

That, however, is but a tendency, and there are counter-tendencies. For the workers now become embedded in a sort of mould—an interacting group with its own private set of social norms and sanctions. The content of these norms will be largely derived, *initially*, from individual experiences in the

[12] See above ch. Two, introduction.
[13] Himmelweit, p. 168.
[14] Leonard Broom and Philip Selznick, *Sociology*, Harper, 1963, p. 117.

factory, and despite the 'compensating service' of the group, those experiences remain to a substantial degree frustrating. Now each individual worker's contribution to the content of the norms will vary not only because individual experiences in the factory are unique but because each worker brings to the factory a unique psychological structure, including a unique capacity to bear frustration. Nonetheless, interaction within the group will bring the varying contributions more or less into line. Distinctive norms develop, which are transmitted to new members and enforced by sanctions. These sanctions are both positive (the rewards of membership) and negative—ranging from teasing and mild rebukes to threats of violence and sending to Coventry. What *is* sanctioned (the norms) may well cut across the planned goals of the factory, as notoriously with restrictive practices. The whole ethos of the group is likely to be restrictive, defensive, obstructive, tending towards a grudging, minimal performance of the set tasks rather than an eager or even a ready cooperation.

Where the balance between these opposing tendencies will settle must vary from industry to industry and plant to plant. In general, by partly serving (up to a point) the workers' root-needs, the primary group will probably have the effect of keeping frustration down and possibly of making the residual frustration a shade more tolerable. Even so, on the evidence of the previous chapter (drawn from industrial contexts where primary groups must be presumed to exist), such residual frustration remains considerable. Now whatever 'quantum' of frustration is, so to speak, left over or made available for distribution as behaviour or action (aggression, absenteeism and the like) will be all the more effectively articulated if a primary group exists. Come what may, except perhaps in special wartime circumstances, the group will protect the individual worker's actions (or responses to frustration). At the same time the group will prove a splendid means of canalizing whatever resentment and aggressiveness remain. It is not simply the power of collective action, at least in the usual sense. It is not simply the demonstrable fact that interaction within a group will produce something like common norms or standards, which, in this instance, will reflect the resentment and aggressiveness, and to which individual workers will conform, as much for the rewards of membership (the capacity of the group to serve root-needs) as for the more publicized punishments, such as sending to Coventry. It is also (recrossing the academic frontier) that group norms tend to be assimilated by the individual members of the group, in whom the norms appear as individual attitudes, or predispositions to act. Group norms and individual attitudes *tend* to match; this is the real significance of the concept of 'internalizing the norms' (so little understood, thanks to the division of academic subjects). And it is this that gives the work-group so much of its subtle power. What is happening at bottom is nothing less than the beginning of the process whose end-product is a certain type of character. Altogether, the conclusion has to be that, in general, the primary group, despite (partly because of) its services, is a disruptive foreign body in the larger social system of the factory, tending to be subversive of the factory's objectives—a certain output at a certain cost or price. It is this aspect, certainly, that strikes the managers once they have been trained to identify groups rather than atoms. Nothing is more understandable than that managers should see primary groups as threats to the satisfaction of their *own* root-needs. To the managers' response and perspective we must now turn, for that constitutes a crucial part of the industrial problem.

CHAPTER SIX

MANAGEMENT'S IMAGE OF THE WORKER

It is surprisingly easy to overlook that managers as well as workers have root-needs to be satisfied. Some of these needs are well attested; for example, managers in countries and social systems as diverse as the United States and Poland are highly motivated by a need for achievement.[1] If that is so, men strongly moved by the need to achieve presumably become managers by self-selection for the career. On the other hand, judging by the biographies of some employer-managers (for example, the strikingly long hours they work), their affiliative need may be less compelling. This is merely speculative. At all events, appearances sometimes to the contrary, managers do belong to the human race and so are as much entitled to the gratification of their needs as anyone else. Certainly if we could so organize industry as to permit the gratification of their highest needs, the whole industrial situation would be radically improved overnight. In Part II we shall discover reason to think that the release of the managers' creative energies is well within our grasp.

Potentially, the manager seems well placed for needs-gratification. Even allowing for regional variations, he is well and often highly paid, and receives generous fringe benefits of one sort or another. Thus some of his biogenic needs are well cared for. Insofar as the need for safety turns on 'controlling' the future, 'top-hat' pensions schemes contribute to it. Insofar as that need turns on power or control over one's working environment, the manager is in a better position than anyone else in the factory to plan ahead and so break through that fear of the unknown which envelops the worker like a dark cloud. As the decision-maker he also seems more in control of

[1] David C. McClelland, *The Roots of Consciousness*, Van Nostrand Insight Book, 1964, pp. 22–3.

the current situation than anyone else in the factory. By virtue of authority and its symbols, he seems likely to satisfy substantially his need for esteem. The senior manager at least seems able to gratify his need for self-fulfilment.

Yet there is a cloud on the horizon, bigger than a man's hand. Apart from rivalry and competition (inside the factory or firm as well as out), wage demands as well as those other demands entering into earnings-drift appear to threaten profits and so in the long run the gratification of many of the manager's own needs. For 'profits', in managerial calculations, are so interpreted as to contribute to the manager's needs for safety or control, esteem and fulfilment, thinking of course not of the money but of the underlying achievement. Similarly, the various behavioural responses of the workers to *their* frustration all present themselves to management as problems and obstacles: aggression not simply in its most overt form but the aggression of the tongue and of 'bloody-minded' behaviour; the systematic thieving, just as systematically rationalized; voluntary absenteeism; labour turnover; apathy, day-dreaming, resignation and so on.

Seeing such threatening behaviour day after day, managers come to regard workers with a mixture of contempt and hostility, and to form an assessment of 'human nature' that is a gross caricature of man. For example, discussing the causes of our comparatively low productivity in recent years, 'a representative group' of British managers laid the blame largely upon their own loss of power to discipline workers during a period of full employment, to the apathy and indifference of workers, and to the desire of workers for more money in return for less effort.[2] For the United States, Douglas McGregor's formulation, Theory X, probably represents much managerial thinking. According to Theory X, man has an inherent dislike of work and will avoid it if he can; he must therefore be coerced into achieving the objectives of the factory; rejecting responsibility, he wants to be controlled and directed, has little ambition and seeks security above all else.[3]

The implied theory of motivation and generally the image of the worker that can be discerned in such characterizations

[2] Chris Argyris, *Personality and Organization*, Harper, 1957, p. 124.
[3] *The Human Side of Enterprise*, McGraw-Hill, 1960, ch. 3.

bear no excessive resemblance to man as the social psychologist and others can more or less show him to be. Why, then, do managers harbour such an image? It is partly, of course, because they see man in the distorting mirror of the factory. In the factory, man's other motivations (i.e. his higher needs), being so substantially frustrated, are not only lost to the managers' sight, so that the worker seems to them almost crippled; in addition the workers' very frustration brings about behaviour that managers find extremely troublesome and threatening; this experience adds to the distortion. Here is the most subtle of distortions, the most vicious of vicious circles. Yet it is not only the managers' current experience that produces a distorted image of the worker. As newcomers to management, they absorb a folk-lore that leads them to expect what they themselves experience. Underlying that managerial folk-lore is a whole intellectual tradition from which three main strands, hopelessly entangled in their industrial application, can be teased out for brief inspection. The first is made up from that individualistic mode of thought which was for so long dominant in so many realms (in philosophy, for example, as well as in psychology, politics and economics) after the Renaissance, Reformation and then the Scientific Revolution of the seventeenth century. The atom is perhaps its most characteristic image-entity. Applied to the industrial situation, the individualistic mode suggests that a factory is composed simply of so many 'isolated' individual workers, or atoms.

The second strand comprises a theory that purports to explain the 'directionality' (Henry Murray's term) of the individual person. During the period 1780–1860 (significantly, the age, approximately, of the Industrial Revolution), 'directionality' was explained primarily in terms of psychological hedonism. According to that theory, which was a species of 'springs' psychology, the only motive sustaining activity and conduct *is* the pursuit of pleasure and the avoidance of pain. To whom this theory, in its modern form, should be attributed is a matter for debate: here it is sufficient to cite the seventeenth-century philosopher, John Locke, for the view that 'happiness and misery are the two great springs of human action'. In the succeeding century, another philosopher, David Hume, declared that 'the chief spring, or actuating principle, of the human mind is pleasure or pain', at least insofar as one calculates rationally in terms of ends. Spanning the eighteenth and nineteenth centuries, Jeremy Bentham, who also thought in terms of the 'springs of human action', kept repeating for some forty years that man's sovereign masters, pain and pleasure, govern us in all we do, in all we say, in all we think. He even constructed a 'felicific calculus' of pleasures and pains. The fourteen simple pleasures and the dozen simple pains were to be scientifically measured by their intensity, duration, certainty or uncertainty, propinquity or remoteness, and, over a long period, their fecundity and purity as well. So fundamental were 'these points, on which the whole fabric of morals and legislation' rests, that Bentham took the trouble later to print a mnemonic verse:

> *Intense*, *long*, *certain*, *speedy*, *fruitful*, *pure*—
> Such marks in *pleasures* and in *pains* endure.
> Such pleasures seek if *private* be thy end:
> If it be *public*, wide let them *extend*.
> Such *pains* avoid, whichever be the view:
> If pains must come, let them *extend* to few.[4]

Bentham needed a felicific calculus in particular because he married psychological hedonism to ethical hedonism—the doctrine that pleasure is the good that one *ought* to pursue. It was already some two thousand years old when Bentham wrote, but in his hands it now became a powerful instrument for institutional and general social reform. Under French inspiration (he himself acknowledged the influence of the French philosopher, Helvétius), Bentham chose as his 'standard of rectitude for actions' their ostensible tendency to 'augment the mass of happiness in the community'. In order to apply this standard of rectitude, however, he needed a measuring instrument: hence the felicific calculus, which he, too, wielded like a sickle (as the historian, Noel Annan, so evocatively said of a latter-day Cambridge economist steeped in the Benthamite tradition).[5]

[4] *An introduction to the Principles of Morals and Legislation*, ed. by Wilfrid Harrison, Blackwell, 1948, p. 151.

[1] Said of Henry Fawcett, Marshall's predecessor in the chair of political economy at Cambridge. Quoted in T. W. Hutchinson, *A Review of Economic Doctrines*, Clarendon Press, Oxford, 1953, p. 10, n. 1. I have drawn much upon this outstanding survey.

None of these founding fathers, not even Bentham (who made a place for sympathy), held to their psychological hedonism without qualification, but as so often their doctrines tended to be swallowed neat. Benthamite doctrine is particularly important for this discussion because it passed into political economy (or economics) in the concept of utility. By the time that Nassau Senior, perhaps the major economist in the period between Ricardo and John Stuart Mill, was giving his inaugural lecture at Oxford (1826), the conception of man as a pleasure-seeking animal had been built into the foundations of political economy. The whole of political economy, he declared, rests upon four self-evident propositions, the first of which is that man is a hedonistic animal. At mid-century the German economist, Hermann Gossen, was trying to make political economy a 'science of enjoyment'.

Partly through the medium of political economy but no doubt by other routes as well, something very like psychological hedonism passed, attenuated, into the employer-manager's stereotype of the individual worker, 'pleasure' being roughly transposed as 'money' or 'wages'. Nor was that all. Man came to be conceived not only atomistically or individually, not only as a pleasure- or money-seeking individual but also as a maximizing individual. This—the third strand—was Bentham's own special contribution; he it was who made the individual maximization of pleasures (or utilities) a crucially important assumption about the behaviour of man.

All three lines converged on the early industrial workshops, where the new emphasis on payments-by-results (in the form of piece-work) well illustrates the whole mode of thought. Already the ground had been prepared, some piece-work schemes having been used (in copper-mining and in the sinking of colliery shafts) from at least the seventeenth century onwards, and in tin-mining from perhaps the fourteenth century. Typically, however, such schemes had been based on the working group, whereas the new ones were directed essentially at the individual worker. As such, piece-work was greeted as a major innovation of the age. By the mid-1830s it had become common in the cotton industry, and was then enshrined as a principle in the work of Charles Babbage, perhaps the first British writer on scientific management, although another half-century passed before his ideas about incentives as part of a general efficiency scheme took a really firm hold.[6] Implicitly or explicitly, the view gained ground among employer-managers that industrial man should be treated as a separate atom, as a pleasure- (or money-) seeking atom and as a rational, pleasure-maximizing atom.

The underlying intellectual tradition has long since been transformed. It has come to be generally realized that 'the natural fact' is the social group rather than the separate atom or individual.[7] Indeed, without interaction in at least a small group, we do not—cannot—become recognizably human; we crawl about on the floor making animal noises. The decline and fall of psychological hedonism may be conveniently dated from the 1870s, when the Cambridge philosopher and economist, Henry Sidgwick, was inventing the term the better to refute the concept, having been himself weaned away from it by reading the criticisms of the eighteenth-century moralist, Bishop Butler, who had taken the wickets but somehow lost the game. While Sidgwick was boring from within the tradition, remaining true to a type of ethical hedonism, other hands at Oxford were preparing to blow it up with gunpowder originally made in Germany. In the traditional phrase, the Rhine (carrying Hegel's thought) flowed into the Thames. Hurrying back from the Oxford Town Hall where he did duty as an elected councillor, T. H. Green launched his attack on hedonism in general, rejecting mere animal wants or 'susceptibilities' as the determinants of behaviour, and insisting on the importance of reason as *the* motive for action. The real Oxford Hegelians, Bosanquet and the recluse Bradley, completed the destruction, at least in the minds of those who could understand them. But the most radical revision was about to come from psychology itself, emerging in the 1860s as a separate discipline. Both Benthamites and their Oxford critics had in common a belief in reason, in the rational man. But when, in 1908, the Lancashire-born Scot, William McDougall came to

[6] S. Pollard, *Economic History Review*, vol. XVI, no. 2, Dec. 1963, pp. 254–71; R. P. Lynton, op. cit., pp. 19, 31, 36.

[7] Bertrand de Jouvenal, 'Du Groupe', *Revue Française de Science Politique*, 5, 1955, pp. 49–62.

publish the pioneering work in social psychology,[8] he traced the springs of human action to the instincts, or inherited tendencies to act. From these come all thought and action, individual and collective. Almost in the words of Hume, intellectual processes are deemed to be the 'servants' of the ends set by the instincts. The prime movers of all human activity, then, are not cognitive (or intellectual) but conative (or impulsive). Pleasure and pain come into it only in the intellectual choice of means selected to serve given ends. That is to say, pleasure and pain are not in themselves motivational.

Such a mode of thought, derived from Darwinian biology, evidently depreciates not only pleasure-seeking man but also in some degree rational man as well. It is not surprising that five years later in Watson's Behaviourism man appears simply as the sum of his instincts, and man's thinking as but a reflection of what he does. Three years later again the Italian sociologist-economist, Pareto was putting his whole weight upon non-logical behaviour in man: he distinguished between *residues* (men's real motives) and *derivations*—plastic bags wrapping up (=explaining, justifying) the non-logical behaviour. Four years later still, in 1920, Freud, whose earlier, pre-McDougall writings had embodied remnants of hedonism, carried the argument 'beyond the pleasure principle'. As, in his work generally, so much of the motivational drive was said to take place below the level of awareness, the assumption of conscious calculation to produce a surplus of pleasures over pains suffered further injury. So, too, did the assumption of *a* conscious calculator. To that extent the conception of a rational man was still further undermined.

Meanwhile, the economists had not been idle. For the purpose in hand, two crucial developments may be distinguished. In the first of these, the theory of (economic) value came to be explained from the side of demand rather than of

[8] *An Introduction to Social Psychology*, Methuen, Oct. 1908; Gordon Allport (in Gardner Lindzey, ed., op. cit., vol. I, p. 9) makes the American, Edward Ross the pioneer, but my copy of his *Social Psychology*, Macmillan, gives Nov. 1908 as the date of first publication.

I am indebted to Allport's survey, 'The Historical Background of Modern Social Psychology', op. cit., ch. I, for much material. Also to Gardner Murphy, 'Social Motivation', in op. cit., Vol. II, ch. 16 and his *An Historical Introduction to Modern Psychology*, Routledge and Kegan Paul, 5th ed., 1949.

supply. The significance of this for our discussion is that emphasis now came to be put (in Manchester and London Universities, Vienna and Lausanne) on the (marginal) *utility*, or *pleasure*, of commodities to the consumer rather than on the *pain* or sacrifice of the producer. Hedonism, so to speak, had crossed the floor. But it was still hedonism: *utility* as *pleasure* was still generally as real as morning jam,[9] and as measurable. The second development consists in the discarding of these assumptions. As a result of work at London University between the 1880s and 1934, the idea of measuring the marginal utility of goods in money terms is abandoned in favour of a comparison by the consumer of the overall satisfaction to be obtained from different bundles or baskets of goods. Thus the marginal rate of substitution—the valuing of one good in terms of another—replaces marginal utility. Meanwhile, in any case, *pleasure* had been squeezed out of *utility*. The transition is strikingly illustrated in the person of Alfred Marshall at Cambridge. Marshall had at first accepted the hedonistic psychology, which (one supposes) he had taught in the 1870s when lecturing on moral and political philosophy for the moral sciences tripos at Cambridge. The first edition of his great work on economics appeared in 1890. In it he made free use of the terms *pleasure* and *pain*. For the third edition, however, five years later, he went through the book deleting *pain* and generally replacing *pleasure* by *satisfaction*, *benefit* or *gratification*. That sums up vividly the changing intellectual climate.

The upshot of those trends, so summarily handled here, has been, as Keynes remarked, to separate the superstructure of economic theory from its original psychological foundations. Whether that does, or should, keep economists awake at night, we need not inquire. The point, rather, is that managerial folk-lore, too, has been separated from its foundations. That is to say, the revolution in philosophy, psychology (including psychoanalysis) as well as in economics has scarcely penetrated the industrial realm. It is true that the declining faith in both Britain and the U.S.A. in the method of payment-by-results[10]

[9] As the American economist P. A. Samuelson said of the English economist, Edgeworth (quoted in Hutchinson, p. 111).

[10] R. R. Hopkins, an experienced personnel manager, in *The Listener*, 10 July 1958, *Labour News from the U.S.*, 27 Jan. 1961.

seems to suggest a managerial awakening to the limitations of its assumptions (an inchoate mixture of psychological hedonism and maximization notions). But this decline is usually traced to other causes, including the introduction of a pace of work no longer dependent on mere brawn and muscle, and a managerial desire for a predictable output rather than one that fluctuates according to the whim of the workers. No doubt the trend is to be welcomed, especially as the less the resort to payments-by-results, the smaller (other things being equal) the tendency to earnings-drift.[11] But there is no evidence that managers generally have yet 'seen through' payments-by-results in a sense germane to the discussion in this chapter.

At all events, managers do have a distorted image of the worker. One of the more important tasks of management education is to correct it (and not to teach a few glossy techniques). For that image has immense significance for industrial relations. It conditions the manager's own behaviour towards the workers. Above all, it affects the way in which the worker regards himself, and that is part of the process by which his own character is formed. In the managerial looking-glass the worker sees himself.

[11] See ch. One

CHAPTER SEVEN

SHAPING THE WORKER'S CHARACTER

From the moment that the young school leaver entered the factory, his character will have been developing. By 'character' here I mean simply a set of attitudes, or dispositions to feel, think and act in certain distinctive ways. It is not to be supposed that *attitudes* exhaust *character*; man is indeed a complex 'piece of work'. But attitudes may be taken to constitute the core of character, or at least a central component of it.

The formation of the worker's character in the factory can be conveniently discussed in terms of adult socialization. This is the process of installing a person in a role, which can be thought of as a bundle of social norms—the expectations (duties and rights) attaching to particular positions. While installation in an occupational role (in a very broad sense) is by no means the whole of adult socialization, it is perhaps its most important element. This importance does not merely reflect the hours spent in or at the factory; it also reflects, so strong is the pressure on men to be good providers, the close connection between occupational role and the husband–father role. The American social theorist, Talcott Parsons, even thinks of occupational role as part of the husband–father role.

At all events, the enactment of an occupational role does leave its mark upon the worker. How deep an etching is cut is difficult to judge. Does adult socialization in the factory produce only superficial cuts? Is the product but a persona, in its original sense of mask, rather than a 'true' modification of character—a mask that is removed at the stroke of 4.45 as the workers rush through the factory gates? Even if the answer were 'yes', I could still argue that once the mask is put on, a certain type of behaviour tends to follow, from which the wider view and loyalty is precluded. I happen to think, however, that the daily enactment of an occupational role entails more than the donning of a mask, and that a sufficiently deep impression is made to justify our regarding the process as a true modification of character. Common experience surely sustains this view. We watch the young schoolmaster growing into Mr. Chips; we watch the clerk 'pigeonholing Creation' (in Auden's unforgettable phrase). There is a persistent tradition, too, from at least John Dewey onwards that an occupational role tends to give rise to an 'occupational psychosis', his peculiar phrase for a 'pronounced character of the mind', a special set of preferences, antipathies, discriminations. 'Professional deformation' and 'bureaucratic personality' are among the other variations on the general idea of a 'trained incapacity'. All in all, there is reason to expect that a man's work does substantially shape or modify his character.[1]

What, then, does the factory 'do' to the worker? Evidently, we must first resolve *factory* into its component parts. With the aid of chapters Three, Five and Six, the question can be re-formulated as: what is the significance for character of the division of labour in detail, of *command*, of the primary-group structure and the managerial image of the worker? In answering that question, we must not neglect, recalling chapter Four, to raise another: what does the worker's habitual response to his own prolonged frustration imply for his own character-development?

The division of labour in detail seems to entail principally that subdivision of learning theory usually labelled 'reinforcement' or 'instrumental'.[2] In this process, stimulus gives rise to response, and the required responses, being rewarded, are reinforced, 'stamped in' more or less automatically. Much of this thinking is based on laboratory experiments with rats. But even those who are most dubious about 'rat psychology' (except for rats) can scarcely deny that *reinforcement* (hedonistic overtones again) is *a* powerful mode of learning even for human beings. Now the division of labour in detail is embedded in a role structure that

[1] See Robert K. Merton, *Social Theory and Social Structure*, Free Press, rev. ed., 1947, ch. Six, for references.

[2] Learning theory represents one of the three general approaches to socialization that might have been drawn on here. I set aside Freudianism as having the least to offer on adult socialization. Symbolic interaction theory might well have been used, especially in discussing the significance of the primary group, but when one incorporates it as an alternative or supplementary interpretation, the text becomes unnecessarily complicated.

is, as usual, buttressed by sanctions—punishments and rewards. What is there *in* the division of labour in detail that gains reward and so reinforcement? Essentially, the rewards are for exercising a few simple manual skills, for accepting narrowness and fragmentation and so for not seeing things through or in the round. The worker, in fact, is comparatively well paid to accept limited horizons, a shrunken world from which the wider community associations and loyalties have been virtually squeezed out. To be comparatively well rewarded for working day after day on very limited, even trivial, tasks must take its toll: the endless repetition of fragmented, blinkered operations tends to make for fragmented, blinkered men.

That tendency will be reinforced by the command structure, for it is this that authorizes and enforces the factory sanctions. But by way of another sub-division of learning theory—*cognitive learning*—we can expect *command* to make its own special contribution to the shaping of the worker's character. This cognitive learning may be, for adults, of more significance than reinforcement. It consists in the painting of 'pictures in the head' (to borrow an old term of Walter Lippman's). Of these, self-perceptions are among the more important. Of the sources of self-perception, a worker's status-role (say, position) in the factory and the treatment he consistently receives from others are important. The essential feature of the worker's position is that it is subordinate and dependent. It is a position that carries no responsibility even for methods in the narrower sense, although the worker may have some influence on these in propitious circumstances, such as a period of full employment. Men perennially treated as dependent and irresponsible in one sense learn to be dependent and irresponsible in every sense. Those who have few opportunities to exercise responsibilities simply do not develop characters marked by a *sense* of responsibility. Regularly treated as a thing to be prodded rather than a person with needs to be expressed, the young worker comes to see himself as someone who does not take initiatives but to whom events happen, who does not take decisions but only actions in response to the decisions of others, who has specific tasks but no general responsibility, who is required, in his work, to think no more of the great issues of public policy to which his contribution is relevant or even crucial than is entailed in just doing his job and keeping his nose clean. Some incidental features of *command* may add a dimension of inferiority to his self-perception: segregation of dining-room and canteen facilities, for instance, even when these are technically convenient. Extremely closely associated in practice to *command* yet analytically distinct, management's image of the worker will also add its deleterious quota to self-perception.

Primary groups may provide the setting and occasion for several kinds of learning by the workers who are members of them. Certainly one type of *social learning* takes place—the assimilation of the social norms of the group. (Here the difficulty of any analysis of an 'on-going' process should be frankly acknowledged. The norms embody elements of individual experience in the factory,[3] and therefore reflect *some prior* learning of *some* sort.) If that type of social learning takes place, it follows that there must be some element of reinforcement learning. For adherence to the group norms is rewarded, the reward coming from whatever it is that the worker gains from the group, such as service of his need for safety (or power) and of his affiliative need. Possibly, too, there is cognitive learning, group membership itself serving to emphasize the worker's subordinate and inferior position in the factory, and inviting, by its oppositional and obstructive tactics, disparaging treatment by management. The group may even independently facilitate the learning process. It is known that learning can be facilitated by emotional arousal, as in the extreme case of 'brain washing'. Not in itself a learning process, it may be auxiliary to one, either cognitive or social. Now, if anywhere in the factory, it is in primary groups that emotion is aroused, garnered, expressed; thus the groups *may* assist whatever learning is under way.

It is at this stage that the question of frustration requires to be raised: will not prolonged frustration itself have some effect on the character of the worker? A plausible answer may be suggested. The regular (if not the easy) satisfaction of one's needs will tend to evoke certain habits of response that gradually leave their mark upon one's character. If, for example, a man's safety need is relatively satisfied, that tends to produce a

[3] See end of chapter Five.

relaxed, assured, confident man.[4] On the other hand since frustration *tends* to induce aggressiveness or pugnacity and to bring into play the various mechanisms outlined in chapter Four, it is conceivable that prolonged frustration would turn such responses into permanent attributes of character.[5] Whether such attributes would be generalized (i.e. observable in almost every situation, so that a man is always aggressive or resigned) would presumably depend in part upon individual psychological development. Such habits of response might, on the other hand, be confined to specific locales, such as the factory. Either way, however, the prognosis for industrial relations would not be good.

The whole process might also be character-forming in another sense. What begins as response can take on a certain autonomy, thus ceasing to be a mere response (or 'means') and acquiring the nature of an independent need (or 'end'). In other words, in the course of responding to the frustration of his root-needs, the worker may develop, for example, *a need* to be aggressive which was 'not there' originally, thus compounding the difficulties of the industrial situation. There is possibly a sense, too, in which some of the biogenic needs, served by money or wages, acquire a certain autonomy. This might happen where even the middle-range, not to mention the higher, root-needs are frustrated. Concentration on one's wage packet (or on the goods that money can buy) might then appear as a kind of acquisitive need. The ensuing complications might be extensive. Since the material goods bought by wages are not simply 'functional' but also confer esteem, these might come to be disproportionately sought after, both absolutely in the form of high wages but also relatively in the form of differentials as against workers deemed to be less skilled or somehow less deserving. The goods might even become part of the worker's 'extended self', or self-perception. Here the need for esteem fuses indirectly with some of the biogenic needs.[6]

These considerations, which take one far from learning theory as conventionally discussed, raise very difficult issues

[4] Maslow, op. cit., p. 114.

[5] Theodore M. Newcomb, *Social Psychology*, Tavistock Publications with Routledge and Kegan Paul, 1952, p. 358.

[6] Cf. D. Krech, R. A. Crutchfield and E. L. Ballachey, op. cit., pp. 73–4.

that I cannot hope to resolve here (or anywhere). If, however, the mere mention of these possibilities emphasizes the absurdity of our current neglect of the character-forming properties of factory life, it will have been valuable. Meanwhile, it seems to me that a useful link with the earlier discussion might come through the facilitative effect of emotional arousal. That is to say, frustration might be most usefully conceived, in this context, as arousing the emotion that assists the learning processes properly so called.

As a crude approximation, then, the factory worker *learns* (chiefly through the division of labour in detail but also from the command structure) to be limited in his horizons and loyalties; *learns* (through *command* and management's image of him) that he is seen as inferior, apathetic, indifferent to almost everything except more money for less effort; *learns* from his primary group to regard himself as not only separate from, but also generally in opposition to, *them* and to *their* plans and intentions. As he learns, so he tends to *be*. Out of the cumulative process comes a tendency to modify the pre-factory *self* of the worker. In other words, the worker acquires, as part of his character, a distinctive set of attitudes, or dispositions (which are presumably finely notched in the central nervous system).

Only detailed inquiry could show these attitudes in their full richness, but the contours stand out fairly clearly. The cognitive, or 'intellectual', element in attitudes (which are usually resolved into three parts) will surely include derogatory views of the plant, factory and firm where so much frustration is experienced; of the shop-floor supervisors and other managers who seem to be the authors of that frustration; of the capitalism under which most enterprises are still carried on. Such persons and entities will be the object of powerful emotions—feelings of dislike at best, outright hostility at worst (the affective element in attitudes). On the other hand, the worker will applaud his primary group, with its practices and code, and see it in—

> 'The light that never was, on sea or land,
> The consecration, and the poet's dream.'

With the intellectual 'stance' and the emotional allegiance go the readiness to act (the behaviour element): to attack at the drop of a hat in the one case; to defend fiercely and if necessary at great sacrifice in the other. Since each of the three components act and react on the others, they tend to form a more or less consistent pattern, although the degree of consistency in any particular person is always a matter for inquiry. In general, attitudes are both fairly coherent and, so to speak, cemented in, being thus particularly hard to dislodge and change.

CHAPTER EIGHT

WORKERS INTO UNIONISTS

It is (workers with) attitudes such as these that form the pith and marrow of trade unions. So far, as a convenient expository device, it has been assumed that the workers are young and inexperienced, the factory new and not yet unionized. In relaxing the last of these assumptions, I make no attempt to chart the transition historically. For that I should have to draw upon a history of trade unionism written from the point of view of sociological social psychology, i.e. showing the sociological—say, occupational—determinants of individual properties, such as attitudes, when and how such properties were 'fed into' this or that union and with what results. Such a history is not available to be pillaged. Accordingly, I make use of a simple typology, which, in any case, is perhaps all that is necessary, or at least all that can be expected, in an essay of modest length.

In the first type there occurs a direct translation of workers-with-certain attitudes into an 'external' association that, in due course, prospers and grows, becoming a 'proper' union without any intervening primary-group stage. For although every factory will harbour a tendency towards primary-group formation, the tendency may not be able to gain ground. Why some factories do not provide a suitable soil for primary-group growth is perhaps not fully understood, the conditions for such growth having been little studied. The emergence of informal structures (of which primary groups are one part) has been the subject of some study; the technology, the layout of the department and the placement of the worker were among the significant factors.[1] These have obvious relevance for

[1] A. Zaleznik, C. R. Christenson and F. Roethlisberger, with G. C. Homans, *The Motivation, Productivity and Satisfaction of Workers*, Harvard University Graduate School of Business Administration, 1958; Zaleznik, op. cit.

primary groups too. The technology, governing, for example, the physical proximity or remoteness of man, must be of major importance. Whatever the reasons, however, we can conceive a direct translation: men-with-attitudes into trade union.

In the second type of translation, the primary group, evidently fostered by the technology and the other prerequisites, dresses up in formal clothes to become the union. Between the informal and the formal probably lies a transitional stage in which quasi-formal leaders (shop stewards in fact) speak in the name of the group. In the formal stage, small local branches are established. These spread out in a web across the country, and eventually, after many vicissitudes, a trade union takes it place in the ranks of the secondary groups of the land. The circle will be complete if, as is likely, the union's rules then provide for the election of shop stewards (under whatever name).

Whatever the route taken, the prognosis for industrial relations is unfavourable. If recruitment into the union is direct, then, since, *initially*, an association must take its colour from its creators, the union will *tend* to reflect the factory-induced attitudes of the workers. The italics are essential as reminders that one should never expect a simple extrapolation from individual attitudes to union norms. The process is not one of addition but of convergence. Here the union situation will be *unstructured*. To it the workers will bring a range of attitudes that have a family resemblance but are not identical. As a result of reciprocal adjustments, however, some common standards or norms are eventually reached. Initially, although no mere summations, these will, in characteristic content, be the correlatives of the individual attitudes: assuming a new union, not an organizing drive by a well-established one, there is nowhere else for the norms to come from at this stage. Thus the union receives as its raw material men whose attitudes to management, to work, almost to life itself, are inimical to good industrial relations and to the wider community view.

Recruitment by way of a conversion of a primary group (or groups) into a union complicates without invalidating this conception.[2] Here the union situation is not unstructured,

[2] Cf. E. Wight Bakke, 'Why Workers Join Unions', in E. Wight Bakke and Clark Kerr, *Unions, Management and the Public*, Harcourt, Brace, 1948, p. 42 and passim.

convergence having occurred earlier in the formation of the primary group itself. One now moves upon a different, more specifically sociological plane. The norms of the union will be, *initially*, the norms of the primary group it replaces. As such, once again, the prospects for industrial relations and for taking a wider community view can hardly be good.

One way or another, there now exists a union, with a local habitation and a name as well as an initial set of norms. The fact that it now has an *external presence* is of crucial significance. The phrase does not refer to the union buildings or to the union's capacity to sue and be sued, but to the end-product of people's unique capacity to objectify their *interactions* as *social groups*. This is W. J. H. Sprott's 'extraordinary quasi-objectivity' of institutions:[3] their seeming to stand outside people although really 'models' in people's heads, comprising shared beliefs, expectations, evaluations and interpretations. Workers now come to see the union as over and above them: listen to the tone of voice in which they speak of 'the *union*' or '*our* union', an entity to be fought for and over, with battle honours (won not only against management but, as they often see it, against the public too), symbols, emotionally-tinged myths, no less potent if ill-founded. This is reification—roughly, making an abstraction concrete; it is very powerful magic.

Meanwhile, under the influence of the external environment (the structure of the industry and of collective bargaining, the strategy and tactics used by employers, etc.), the union norms will have been developing. To the original building some new rooms will be added. For instance, a norm of solidarity, or sticking shoulder to shoulder, especially in trial and adversity, will develop. The pristine simplicity of the earlier picture now fades a little, for a new norm will tend to re-define individual needs (and attitudes): in this instance, something like a need-for-the-union-to-survive emerges as the correlative of the norm of solidarity. How far the process of re-definition can go, and what exactly will be the relationship between the ultimate needs and the newer ones, are very difficult questions. It seems plain, however, that the new needs must fit into the place available in the whole matrix of root-needs. Thus the new need for union survival ought probably to be regarded as an

[3] *Sociology at the Seven Dials*, Athlone Press, London, 1962, pp. 4–5.

intermediate need serving ultimate needs. (Alternatively it might be interpreted as a goal—that pattern of implied action appropriate to satisfying ultimate needs). At the sociological level, it is surely absurd to suppose that a union's emergent norms can, in the long run, get very far out of line with the individual root-needs of its members. A norm of solidarity is appropriate to the survival of the union, and the survival of the union is important, in the long run, only because the union serves individual root-needs. At any given time, some norms may be out of line with individual needs (and attitudes), but in general a 'strain towards consistency' must be expected to induce a substantial measure of consonance between them. But somehow or other, by ways no doubt devious and obscure, admitting always the possibility of temporary divergencies, union norms must serve union men.

We would never think otherwise if we remembered that *the union* (the group, institution, society) has no independent existence apart from the beliefs that constitute it; it is a model, or picture in the head. Sprott's warning ought to be hung like a religious text in every sociologist's bedroom: 'Reification is the besetting temptation to sociologists'.[4] That is the truth and the light; once we see it, we will no longer swallow the view that somehow union norms (still less, the so-called union needs) can live for long 'detached' from men—striving, swarming, demanding men—and *their* needs. To serve these is what a union is *for*.

At all events, we can agree that, whatever the status and significance of the emergent norms, these are unlikely to sweeten industrial relations or to foster the wider community view. Thus, even if the norm of solidarity were regarded as somehow 'detached', it obviously serves to harden the lines between the men who *are* solid and the employer-managers and even the public at large. This must apply, it would seem, to all emergent norms. Accordingly, the cumulative effect of the formation of the union is to emphasize differentiation and almost to glorify separateness.

Here, of course, as so often throughout this essay, I resort to a 'model' (or typology); the extent to which any identifiable

[4] ibid., p. 12. Since Sprott is both sociologist and psychologist, his warning should be taken all the more seriously.

union fits the model is always a subject for investigation. We know, for instance, from the work of Arnold Tannenbaum and Robert Kahn that American unions show much variation in 'adherence to norms and observance of rules'.[5] More generally, since I derive the model from current motivations and current industrial and other conditions, I neglect Time. So it is undoubtedly true that I neglect the surviving unions of an earlier age, specifically the status-conscious unions of craftsmen founded or developed during the nineteenth century.[6] How the introduction of that factor would blur the outlines of the scene I have sketched may be judged from Leonard Sayles's researches in the American motor car industry. He studied the trimmers working on a sub-assembly line; they are responsible for the 'soft goods' such as door pads and wind hose. Traditionally they had used tacks and hammers, but although management had introduced a stapler gun in substitution, they persisted in thinking of themselves as upholsterers, i.e. as craftsmen, superior to mere assemblers and worthy of a 'differential', which, although small, was conceded.[7] The general importance of this factor is difficult to judge. In Britain, for instance, the United Patternmakers' Association stands out partly because it is one of the few remaining 'real' craft unions, which for 'many' years have been experiencing a relative decline.[8] What, in fact, *is* the distribution of craft attitudes throughout British unions as a whole today? We do not know and the results of an inquiry might surprise us. However, I do not take my stand on that ground; craft ideology doubtless survives. On the other hand, its survival does not, I submit, invalidate the model, which is not designed to 'represent' British unionism as such but only to 'capture' or isolate enough of it to explain the behaviour of many workers in industry and the shaping of their personalities there. In the last resort, the questions are: does the model illuminate the

[5] Arnold S. Tannenbaum and Robert L. Kahn (Survey Research Centre, University of Michigan), *Participation in Union Locals*, Row, Peterson, 1958, p. 204.

[6] H. A. Clegg, Professor of Industrial Relations at the University of Warwick, private comment.

[7] Leonard R. Sayles, *Behaviour of Industrial Work Groups*, John Wiley with Chapman and Hall, 1958, pp. 28–30.

[8] H. A. Clegg, A. J. Killick and Rex Adams, *Trade Union Officers*, Harvard University Press, ch. 2, esp. pp. 16–17.

observed behaviour or facts? Is it explanatory and to that degree predictive? I think that the argument from chapter Two onwards, with its resort to models, does illuminate what I set out to illuminate, but that, of course, I have to leave to others to judge for themselves.

In time, then, the union develops a code, partly crystallized in the rule-book, partly embodied in oral traditions. This code represents what the American social scientist, W. I. Thomas called 'the definition of the situation'. At any given period it will have a specific content or substance: thus at the Standard Motor Company in Coventry (makers of the 'Triumph' cars), the code was designed to eliminate 'predatory competition' between workers. It also prescribed that overtime should be shared, that employment should be kept stable even at the cost of some adjustment in the production bonus, and much else besides.[9] Violation of any part of the code provokes emotional protests, which cause the offenders pain: they will be called, as appropriate, coward, traitor, heretic, scab, rat.[10] Even codified acts of no intrinsic importance come eventually to be 'saturated with emotion'. Definitions, however arbitrary, that are embodied in the habits or traditions of a union come to be regarded as right. In other words, the union provides its own authoritative definition of civic obligation and virtue.

It follows that the union code *tends* to re-define the individual attitudes of its members. Since attitudes are a central element in character, the union might almost be said to make members in its own image. But there are distinct limits to that. Just as the union cannot (I believe) re-make the matrix of individual needs at will, so the union cannot hand out attitudes on a platter. Attitudes arise out of the reception accorded to a man's root-needs, and are anchored by those needs. The process is, really, reciprocal. The union code will tend to change individual attitudes, but individual attitudes continually pass into the code. The whole problem under discussion cannot be understood, much less 'solved', unless it is realized that

[9] Seymour Melman, *Decision-Making and Productivity*, Blackwell with John Wiley, 1958, pp. 82–4.

[10] 'The Persistence of Primary-Group Norms in Present-Day Society' in Herbert S. Jennings, *Suggestions of Modern Science Concerning Education*, Macmillan, New York, 1910 (inside page gives Oct. 1917), pp. 100–9.

irresponsible attitudes flow into the union code as a tidal river into the sea.

That, of course, is not how it appears to the trade unionist. For a profound transformation has now taken place, convincingly sketched by Frank Tannenbaum at the beginning of the 1950s but still little understood. The union becomes not simply or primarily a vehicle for various mundane purposes, although that is what it often appears to be: with its normative structure (or code) it becomes rather a 'symbolic universe', replacing that undermined by the Industrial Revolution. For the break-up of the older pattern of simple loyalties and understandings is 'the great moral tragedy of the industrial system', which unwittingly 'destroyed the symbolic and meaningful world that had endowed the life of the individual with an ethical character'. The significance of a trade union is that it represents an attempt, for the most part unconscious, to re-create *in itself* that pre-Industrial Revolution society in which the worker had, despite all else, a recognizable and accepted place, and in which his life had meaning because he shared with others a common code. The union *itself* embodies the old symbolic universe (so far as that is reproducible); it is a social and ethical system, not merely an economic one: it is concerned with the whole man; its ends are 'the good life'.[11]

This conception of a trade union as a moral universe is, I believe, of profound importance. It is also, however, more complex than Tannenbaum makes it appear: precisely because of his wish to bring out the significance of institutionalization, he leaves an impression of a union not only as a moral universe but also as a homogeneous one. On the contrary (as he himself does not need to be told), a union operates on at least two moral levels. For the creation of a union does not destroy the informal structure from which (as we may again suppose) it sprang: what happens is the superimposition of the formal upon the informal, corresponding to which there appear to be, on occasion at least, two moral domains. This complication comes to light, I should say, in some 'wildcat' strikes, those spontaneous strikes not led or authorized by union officials, who lose face in consequence. Alvin Gouldner's study of such

[11] *A Philosophy of Labour*, Knopf, pp. 7–8, 10–11.

a strike in the United States[12] discloses that it was neither a calculated move in a crude struggle for power, as management not unnaturally thought, not merely an outburst of emotion, but an expression of moral indignation. For their 'walk-out', which was tantamount to a criticism of their own union as well as of management, the workers felt moral justification. Thus the union at that time was not a morally homogeneous unit but divided into two sections at least.

What underlay this 'wildcat' strike, in fact, was the frustration of certain *legitimate* expectations (and the weakness at the time of the grievance machinery for coping with the consequent tension). Of course, satisfaction in full is not to be looked for; in the language of Talcott Parsons, Ego (worker in relation to foreman, say) will look to Alter (the worker's 'reciprocal' at the 'other end' of that relationship, i.e. the foreman) for performance within a certain range. Beyond that range, violations will induce tension and strain. That is what generated this 'wildcat'. For the many dimensions of the problem, Gouldner's work should be itself consulted, but one factor that came into play was *incongruity*, where Ego and Alter have mutually inconsistent expectations. In producing the tension that led to the 'wildcat', many variations were played upon the theme of efficiency *v.* seniority as a criterion for promotion. The details do not concern us here; what counts is that the workers felt their legitimate expectations to have been violated. To that extent it was a moral issue, although management completely failed to see it in that light, and even the union itself was evidently divided.

A 'wildcat' strike at Shaftsbury, Vermont, at the end of October, 1965, in defiance of a contract signed only the previous April, seems to have turned very much upon this issue of seniority *v.* efficiency. One morning some eight out of ten of the workers at the Eagle Square Manufacturing Company, members of Local 645 of the Upholsterers International Union (UIU), just walked off the job. The company's intention was that where two or more applicants for a production job had equal qualifications, then the one with the longer company service would receive preference. The workers wanted greater weight given to seniority. A compromise settlement

[12] *Wildcat Strike*, The Antioch Press, 1954.

was reached whose very elaborateness indicated the importance of the issue. Under the new procedure (which did not cover the highly skilled grades), the company would post a notice of a vacancy and make a selection from the candidates. If they chose a relatively junior man, they would explain their reasons to a special union committee. If the committee objected, the more senior man who had been passed over would be given a trial extending from ten working days to four weeks. His performance would then be evaluated. His position might be confirmed; on the other hand, management might want to return him to his former position (and rate of pay) and substitute their original choice. If the local union still disagreed, the dispute would go to arbitration. No wonder the UIU business representative for southern Vermont and New Hampshire commented after the settlement of the two-day strike: 'I hope a negotiation like this doesn't come up every day.'[13]

Now there is no evidence at all to show how far, if at all, the workers were entitled, on this score, to have formed expectations that they must be presumed to have regarded as legitimate. But it seems not unreasonable to add this instance as an illustration to reinforce Alvin Gouldner's analysis. Of the general point, at least, there can be no doubt: a union is by no means invariably a homogeneous moral entity and may on occasion divide into parts. Thus *incongruity* may arise in the special form of inconsistency between parts of a union conceived in moral terms. Caught in such a web of confusion, the full-time union official as well as the foreman may play Alter to the local worker's Ego.

Yet, either as parts or as wholes in this sense, the new creation, the union, all too obviously does possess, as the latent consequence of organization, substantial power to disrupt the community. Even with a 'wildcat' the norms of the union come into play to support it; thus, other workers will not be allowed to fill the strikers' jobs.[14] But in favourable circumstances the union will exercise the formidable power that comes from establishing procedures and disciplines for both worker and work, as well as from sheer bargaining strength. Here is a new Leviathan.

[13] *Bennington Banner* (Vermont), 30 Oct. 1965.

[14] Sayles, ibid.

CHAPTER NINE

THE PROBLEM STATED

As we are all members of overlapping social groups, the general issue is the right ordering of our several loyalties. The particular perennial problem, granted full employment, is to persuade trade unions, and hence trade unionists, to recognize themselves as part of an enduring whole, and to secure that right ordering of their several loyalties which, in relation to the just claims of the State acting for the community, is, at its highest, civic virtue. This has a moral dimension, well caught in the Keynesian phrase, 'the widening of the ambit of men's altruism'. The contemporary form of the perennial problem is to persuade the unions, and hence trade unionists, to keep not only their wage claims but above all their actual earnings within the annual increase in the output of goods and services. Thus, under full employment, the focus is on the factory, where men bestir themselves to lever up the nationally-agreed rate with little regard for what even their own national leaders think should be done. This, too, is where 'industrial relations' are made, or marred.

Far from promoting civic virtue, the present industrial organization makes it impossible. Into the factory (a convenient term for all industrial and commercial establishments, including the larger commercial offices) come the young workers with their characters (or selves) already partly formed. Such characters embody certain root-needs, sociogenic as well as biogenic, which, complicated by their capacity for development, require gratification, and to a certain extent in working time, not after hours. Thus the root-needs for safety (or control) and for affection (or belongingness) cannot be put into cold storage until the end of the working day. But every factory as now organized exhibits that 'division of labour in detail' of which Marx wrote; every factory as now organized is a structure of command, as Marx almost wrote, and as Engels well understood. As such, every factory as now organized denies workers the satisfaction of a high proportion of their root-needs. Management and men will in any case disagree about the distribution of the product (or profits); such disagreement now comes to be compounded by the effects of the workers' frustration, making rational solutions more difficult. Some, perhaps much, frustration has constructive results, but in the factory situation, since the obstacles can scarcely be overcome under the existing arrangements, it tends to be frustration 'without hope'. This has certain consequences for the character and behaviour of the worker. They suffer an increase of tension, indicated by pulse rate, blood pressure, and so on; strong emotions, such as anger and rage, fear and anxiety, are aroused. To frustration 'without hope', certain responses, cunningly interwoven in practice, are to be expected: these include aggression (or pugnacity); displacement (or finding a scapegoat); projection; rationalization; and repression, as well as the various forms of withdrawing 'from the field': voluntary absenteeism, labour turnover, apathy and resignation, day-dreaming at work. Observable patterns of behaviour in industry seem to correspond to these expected responses. The true cost to the community must be enormous.

Meanwhile the workers' half-conscious striving to gratify their root-needs continues by other means. One consequence is the formation, where the factory technology permits, of primary groups. Insofar as these afford an alternative mode of satisfying the lower and middle-range root-needs (for safety and affiliation, say), they will tend to reduce any particular level of frustration and to make the remainder more bearable. On the other hand, the primary groups will develop their own norms, whose content comes, initially, from individual experiences in the factory. Despite the compensating 'service' rendered by the group, those experiences still bear the stigmata of much, even great, frustration. Thus primary-group norms are only too likely to be restrictive, defensive, anti-management. Where the balance between these opposing influences will be struck is a matter for investigation; from the literature it seems likely that the primary group is subversive of the larger objectives of the factory. The norms of the group *tend* to be reflected in the individual attitudes of members: the more that happens, the less the need for sanctions, especially punishments. The workers' characters, in other words, are beginning to be shaped.

On workers with such developing characters, managers cast a baleful eye. For they, too, have root-needs, whose gratification is threatened at almost every point by the men: by their wage and other claims and by their *own* behaviour in response to their *own* frustration. Thus managers come to see workers in a peculiarly unfavourable light. This is all the more convincing to them because a whole intellectual tradition has prepared them for what they perceive. Taught to expect men to be not only pleasure- (or money-) seeking animals but also pleasure-maximizing animals, they can see behaviour that ostensibly validates the conception. But this is not because it is the nature of man but only man's nature in a particular type of situation, the rest of his attributes being dormant, 'screened out' by certain features of that situation. If in time the discovery of the primary-group structure and its latent functions (e.g., restrictive practices) cannot be kept even from the least perceptive manager, the reality shock may be all the greater. The groups will be seen as menacing still more the managers' own gratification.

Meanwhile, the workers have been undergoing adult socialization. This entails a number of processes whose status and inter-connection are not fully understood. It seems likely, however, that the workers will learn, through the rewards of the division of labour in detail, reinforced by the command structure, to exercise but a few skills, and to accept a world of limited horizons and loyalties. As his work and situation is, so will he tend to be as a person, i.e. he will exhibit in his 'nature' the central features of his life's activity. Through another learning process (the cognitive) that may be of greater importance than reinforcement-through-reward, workers develop certain self-perceptions. Subordinate, dependent, segregated (as in canteens), wearing perhaps a distinctive dress (overalls), fundamentally irresponsible, they tend to accept the implied valuations, and to *be* the implied persons. The managerial image of the worker may add to the particular tendency. These tendencies are probably underwritten by the learning processes that go on within the primary group, which, through emotional arousal, may facilitate learning generally. It is conceivable that the strong emotion accompanying frustration serves the same purpose. Prolonged frustration might perhaps make its own direct impact on character through regular habits of response, thus conceivably giving rise to a new individual need, e.g. to be pugnacious. That, however, is problematic. The general conclusion is that men tend to become in character what they are daily required to be.

These conclusions can be expressed by saying that in the factory men acquire propensities or inclinations—dispositions to respond to certain other people (foremen, the boss) and other objects in certain ways, e.g. aggressively. These propensities will react upon their cognitions (yielding 'pictures in the head') and feelings. Subtle patterns of feelings, cognitions and propensities will yield interlocking sets of social attitudes, cemented in by powerful emotions. These social attitudes will not be identical in all workers but the substance will be similar. Such attitudes will be inimical to good industrial relations, and preclude the wider view by prescribing a narrow one.

Directly or indirectly, men with these attitudes (or characters) are recruited into the unions. If the translation is then by convergence in an unstructured situation, some common norms are reached in the union. These norms must initially reflect the disgruntled attitudes. If the translation is indirect, then initially the primary-group norms will be taken over as the union norms. One way or another, the union norms will militate against good industrial relations and shut out civic virtue. The union now acquires an identity: by the 'perceptual fallacy', it stands over and above the individual member, claiming, demanding—a brooding coercive presence that may demand sacrifices. In rubbing up against its external environment, the union's norms will develop, but these emergent ones would seem to be anchored in the root-needs of the workers, in the long run. Even if that is not so, the emergent norms will not assist the discharge of civic obligation; on the contrary, they will tend towards irresponsibility.

The union now has a fairly developed code, which for its members 'defines the situation'. The code, only partly written down, will include authoritative definitions of civic obligation, although not under that name. This code 'hits back' on attitudes, within certain limits, but the influence is reciprocal, not one-way. Irresponsible attitudes, being continually created, keep on finding their way into the union code. Thus the union code will be irresponsible too, i.e. it will shut out the wider community view. In itself it symbolizes not only Mill's standing feud between 'the class of capitalists and the class of labourers', but almost between the union and the public at large. That, however, is an observer's view, not the union's; the union conceives itself to be, if not quite the public at large, then a very special public, based, according to one suggestive interpretation, upon a re-creation of the 'symbolic universe' torn apart by the Industrial Revolution. As such, the union constitutes a moral universe, less homogeneous than it at first glance appears but of great force all the same in favourable circumstances.

In groping towards the light, I touch various possibilities. In principle, the problem could be abolished, rather than solved, by a suitable Government policy to eliminate full employment. As *The Times* once wrote in a moment of brazen candour, the 'first function of unemployment' is to maintain 'the authority of master over man'.[1] With a large enough pool of unemployment, national wage claims would be moderated and earnings-drift would become as negligible a problem as it was between the wars. Generally, power would ebb away from the shop stewards to the union centre (or headquarters). I oppose the policy for two reasons. If it is too rhetorical now to say, with Beveridge, that 'a civilized community must find alternatives to *starvation* for the preservation of industrial discipline and efficiency', I think still that 'the essence of civilization is that men should come to be led more by hope and ambition and example and less by fear'.[2] Secondly, full employment, by imposing thought upon us, could lead to a marked improvement in the quality of our industrial life. Nothing more need be said since the policy is politically impossible: political strategy must reject what economics (or one brand of it) whispers.

Theoretically, one can just conceive of a nation-wide scheme

[1] William H. Beveridge, *Full Employment in a Free Society*, Allen and Unwin, 1944, p. 195.

[2] ibid., p. 198. Italics added.

of early socialization designed to modify man's root-needs, so that the pre-factory character of the young workers entering the factory would be less demanding. But this hardly seems worth considering. The only policy at this level is 'dissociation': the workers 'contract out' from any expectation of needs-satisfaction inside the factory. It is supported not only by the French psychologist, Stoetzel,[3] but to some extent by two of the very few experienced industrialists who have shown signs of understanding the problem. Glenn Gilman, of the Lockheed Corporation, concludes that everyone cannot have satisfying relations on the job. Even more relevantly, Lewis E. Lloyd, of Dow Chemicals, who actually accepts Maslow's theory of motivation, concludes that commercial organizations are designed primarily to meet only the first two category of needs within the factory. For the rest workers have to look outside.[4] In varying degrees, therefore, Gilman and Lloyd are 'dissociationists'. But I doubt whether man's needs can be taught not to express themselves wherever the man happens to be; working *is* living. If so, 'dissociation' is tantamount to a confession of failure, condemning us to continue accepting indefinitely the consequences of failure.

Granted that the root-needs are 'on-going' and require a high degree of gratification at work, the next possibility might be to strike at the obstructions that now stand in the way there, giving rise to frustration. The obstructions comprise the division of labour in detail and above all the structure of command. The impact of the former could be reduced by job enlargement, but only marginally, assuming that we want to keep at least our present standard of living. *As usually discussed*, that applies also to radical modifications of the structure of command, but here the issue is far more complicated. From the French social theorist, St.-Simon (through the German sociologist, Max Weber) to such moderns as the English management writer, Lyndall Urwick, a powerful tradition suggests that *the organization* (of which *command*, as the term is here used, is the main component) has to be regarded almost as an absolute. Impressed (as who is not?) by the great and urgent communal

[3] Knowles, p. 216.

[4] Cited in Delbert C. Miller and William H. Form, *Industrial Sociology*, Harper and Row, 2nd ed., 1964, pp. 629–30.

tasks in modern large-scale societies, such writers pin their hopes on the capacity of *the organization* to surpass the limitations of the individual. In Urwick, the tradition finds expression as—

> 'The idea that organizations should be built up round and adjusted to individual idiosyncrasies, rather than that individuals should be adapted to the requirements of sound principles of organization, is as foolish as attempting to design an engine to accord with the whimsies of one's maiden aunt rather than with the laws of mechanical science.'[5]

Although in context that does not go unqualified, I do not accept the notion, for reasons that will become apparent later. All the same, I think that the 'organismic' school[6] underrates the very great achievements of *organization* (or, in the technical sense, bureaucracy): it has its social costs, previously neglected, but without it many of us might well go hungry and uncared for. In any case, it seems certain that 'organismic' (more or less, 'free-range') management could be used only on a very limited scale. If so, it does not provide an escape route from our dilemma.

Granted these arguments (and their predecessors), we have no further stopping-place until we come upon the union code itself. Although they give no sign of realizing it, successive Governments, in appealing for wage restraint, are really trying to change the union code. How very convenient it would be if major problems could be solved so readily, so painlessly, so inexpensively. Would we expect one of those good county regiments to change its code quickly, or at all, at the request of strangers? Or even of its most commanding officer? The code does not belong to any officer but to the regiment. So, too, with the union. The code is union property ('quasi-objectivity' again) and changeable, if at all in the short run, only by the members as a whole and not by the full-time officials, and then only by serious discussions on the part of members, not by lectures from on high.[7]

Even suppose that, by waving a wand, some charismatic

[5] In L. Gulick and L. Urwick, *Papers on the Science of Administration*, Columbia University, New York, 1937, p. 85.

[6] See ch. Three.

[7] Dorwin Cartwright and Alvin Zander, *Group Dynamics*, Row, Peterson, 1st ed., 1953, passim, or almost any text-book on social psychology.

(or magnetic) union leader could transform the code overnight in such fashion as to win *genuine* acceptance on a particular day for a wage-restraint or incomes policy, or some other major national issue, from all his current members. Taking the common static view, we should then declare that the new code would be internalized. Subject to the various limitations, individual attitudes would *tend* to come into line with the new code. But that is not equilibrium: the frustrations of new members (assuming that the factory situation is unchanged) will influence the code. As many unions have a turnover of membership ranging from the substantial to the enormous, that 'influence' would be exerted the very morning after the postulated transformation of the code. Even existing members, in similar circumstances, would find their verbal acceptances immediately under pressure, for the frustration of their needs would continue as before, thus setting in motion that subtle and complex process leading to dispositions-to-respond through attitudes to the union code. We really must stop telling ourselves that there is an easy way out: with fundamental social problems, we have to begin at the beginning. The union code *can* be changed, but not by siren calls, still less by strident demands. If we really want responsible behaviour in industry, we had better start providing the conditions in which it can slowly grow and flourish.

PART II

Towards industrial responsibility

CHAPTER TEN

'FREE BUT RESPONSIBLE' GROUPS

In discussing industrial reform, we must first be quite clear in our minds not only that the traditional approaches are irrelevant but why they are irrelevant. Public ownership, or nationalization, is one such approach. Insofar as it is intended to satisfy the root-needs of the workers, as distinct from serving some broader economic or political purpose, nationalization obviously fails. It fails because, like the private industry it replaced, it rests on the division of labour in detail and on *command*, even though the sharp outlines of *command* are blurred by constitutionalism in the form of joint consultation. Accordingly, most of the workers are as doomed to frustration as if they were still in private industry.

Much the same may be said of syndicalism, which, as 'workers' control', also glossed over the realities of the division of labour in detail and of *command*. Having done so, it forfeits any right to further consideration. Schemes that recognized those realities, however, fail on other grounds. Profit-sharing was one of the earliest of these; in isolation, it fails because it serves only the biogenic needs. Combined with co-partnership (interpreting that vague term to mean some sort of workers' association with managerial decision-making), profit-sharing probably fares rather better, but the number of workers who can be so associated is so small that the general position is unaffected. Joint consultation, in its Whitley and other forms; co-determination, as practised in West Germany; and Workers' Councils, as in Yugoslavia—all these are well-meaning attempts to engage the interest and concern of the ordinary industrial worker. As such they deserve some marks—but not too many, for it ought now to be clear what is wrong with them all. In their different modes, they probably do secure or guarantee the lower root-needs of most or perhaps all workers under their roof, i.e. they serve the biogenic and some of the sociogenic needs, such as the need for safety. They also give those workers who are called upon to play a representative part (in works' councils or even on governing bodies) some satisfaction of their *own* higher root-needs, such as perhaps the need for affection and, very likely, for esteem and self-fulfilment (or achievement). But with the best will in the world (not always displayed or exerted by management), not one of these arrangements can gratify the higher root-needs of the ordinary worker. His interests are not engaged; he is still acted upon rather than acting, if probably finding himself in a stronger general position by virtue of being represented. More secure in his lower needs, he remains substantially frustrated despite all the worthy attempts to make him part of the enterprise.

In this context, then, the traditional approaches fail either because the problem was misconceived or even entirely glossed over, or because workers' motivation was neglected or simply ignored. Only Guild Socialism carried within itself the seeds of growth. At first it might seem to be little more than a gentlemanly English version of French syndicalism. It was far superior to it, however, not only in not wasting breath talking about revolutionary seizures that would never get beyond the seizure of the coffee cups or the breaking of a few wine bottles (prudently emptied first), but also in recognizing the inevitability of a structure of command in industry, and above all (as against joint consultation and co-determination as well), in attempting to grapple with the problem of motivation. It was the earlier Guild Socialists, Orage and S. G. Hobson, who saw in the National Guilds for administering industry the institutions that would 'give free scope to noble motives'.[1] At that stage (1912–13), G. D. H. Cole, although he had been a reader from 1906 of the journal *New Age* in which these ideas were aired, did not call himself a Guildsman; but after he did style himself so (early 1914), he, too, emphasized motives. In a passage soon to be made obsolete, apparently, by the ending of the post-war boom in November 1920, he wrote: 'The real question in industry today is a question of *motive*', and went on to ask what motive the community was going to rely on in future. At

[1] S. G. Hobson, ed. by A. R. Orage, *National Guilds*, Bell, 3rd ed., 1919, Part II, ch. XI, 'Motive under the Guild'.

present the social system is so ordered for employers as 'to throw the main stress and reliance upon the motive of personal greed.' The workers, on the other hand, are manipulated through fear: fear of hunger, of unemployment, of submersion in the hopeless strata of society. Or, rather, they have been so manipulated; but now the self-confident unions have arrived, and the workers in the great industries 'are no longer afraid enough' to continue production under the old system. Accordingly, we have to visualize another system, a choice of system being 'always primarily and fundamentally a choice, not of the machinery to be created, but of the motives to which the principal appeal is to be made'. Cole looked to the principle of 'free service', instead of greed and fear; foresaw an appeal to ideals, not to 'men's material desires and terrors.'[2]

How well this passage anticipates post-1940 Britain, where once again the British worker has ceased to be 'afraid enough'. This concern for motivation puts Guild Socialism, however weak in its details, streets ahead of the other schools of industrial reform. It is illuminating, indeed, to set the Orage-Hobson 'Working Model' of a Guild as visualized half a century ago beside Maslow's theory of motivation. Under the Guild Socialist model, man's physiological (or biogenic) needs would be (in principle) better served: workers would get more than their current wages, perhaps three times more (thanks to greater efficiency and to a 'plus' sum derived from there being no time lost through unemployment). Safety needs would be better cared for because the fear of unemployment would disappear with 'the slow starvation of a competitive wage'. Workers, too, would be cared for in sickness, distress, and old age. Indeed, for Guild Socialists, it is this maintenance and protection of Guild members that really constitutes 'the social revolution'. Affiliative needs would be served because helping one's neighbour in distress is the mark of belonging, or, in their language, of fellowship. The Guild was to be essentially a fellowship as well as an economic organization. Esteem (in the sense of favourable opinion, or respect) would come through self-fulfilment (or achievement). The tradition of craftsmanship, still kept alive, despite 'intense specialization', by the 'companionable nature of the workers', would flourish again.

[2] G. D. H. Cole, *Chaos and Order in Industry*, Methuen, 1920, pp. 17–21.

The workers, among the most poorly paid of whom Orage-Hobson saw 'innumerable signs of genius', are now thwarted because 'their rightful positions go to the blood relations of their employers'; they are denied the satisfaction of achievement. But under the Guild organization 'every private carries a marshal's baton'.[3]

The correspondence between these (in the original) unsystematic thoughts of the Guild Socialists and Maslow's theory of motivation (as also the Argylean triad)[4] is arresting. Weak in other respects, the Guild Socialists were on the right lines with their motivational ideas. But that is not all. They saw as well that the problem is to satisfy the needs of all the members of the Guild, including (in Cole at least)[5] those of the managers. But how was that to be accomplished? Here again their fundamental organizational idea contained the seeds of growth. The widespread needs-satisfaction that they anticipated was to be attained in the Guilds. Now a Guild could serve needs well precisely because it was a semi-independent entity, operating within (as we should now say) an overall national plan. Each Guild would be a sort of inner ring within a larger circle. So long as it conformed to the broad national plan, each Guild would be left to work out its own salvation, and thus enjoy a special kind of participation which would also be a special (and valuable) kind of freedom. Appropriately enough for an entity whose inspiration was originally medieval, the Guild would resemble a 'liberty': a more or less autonomous area or realm, the functional equivalent of the liberties granted to the towns by medieval kings in the form of a charter. Of course, the king, or his modern equivalent, would remain as goal-setter and co-ordinator of the Guilds for the country as a whole.

No doubt there were conceptual difficulties in these Guild Socialist ideas, which in any case never got off the ground. Cole continued his advocacy into the early 1920s, but, like other species of pluralism, Guild Socialism hardly recovered from the accelerated State collectivism of the 1914–18 War period: it was pulverized, as a contemporary said, by the

[3] ibid., also part II, ch. Four, A Working Model.

[4] See ch. Two.

[5] *Guild Socialism Re-Stated*, Parsons, 1920, p. 57.

Defence of the Realm Acts. Yet from it we can extract the notion of 'liberties' as the only practicable way of satisfying the workers' root-needs on the spot. What we have to do is to apply the idea of a Guild or 'liberty' *within* the factory: that is, demarcate a (perhaps variable) realm of independent decision which will stand in relation to management as the Guild under Guild Socialism would have stood in relation to the Government of the day. In some industries the technology might be an absolute bar, but in general it is surely not beyond the wit of industrial man, armed with computers, modern accounting methods and other devices, to 'deconcentrate' some power to the primary groups. One says 'deconcentrate' rather than 'decentralize' in order to make it clear that the broad strategic decisions would still be made by management. Management, however, would so deconcentrate its powers that ordinary workers themselves would have scope to think and act. They would have to keep within the factory plan and budget, but would be left free to draw their own inferences as to the allocation of duties and rights, and possibly arrange the division of the earnings. This, accompanied perhaps, as part of the factory plan by some mitigation of the division of labour in detail, i.e. by some job enlargement, would transform the ordinary worker's situation. He would have opportunities for satisfying his higher root-needs never before open to him under either public or private ownership. His affiliative needs would be far better served in the very process of arranging the work and freely co-operating with others. Esteem, or respect, would come from the contribution freely made. In general, his abilities no longer frozen, he would be free to exercise his 'conscious and unconscious need for mental activity', the denial of which is 'certainly' (an experienced French trade unionist affirms) 'one of the causes of social unrest, if not the most important'.[6] In Maslow's terms, the worker would be able to satisfy his need for self-actualization (or self-fulfilment). This greater satisfaction of root-needs would come to be reflected in less aggressive dispositions to respond to other people, and generally in more constructive and helpful individual attitudes, and ultimately in more constructive primary-group norms and union codes. All

[6] Hyacinthe Dubreuil, *Industrial Organization on the Basis of Autonomous Groups*, International Labour Office, Geneva, 1951, p. 10.

along the line, other things being equal, a chain of reactions wholly favourable to good industrial relations could be expected to follow.

Thus, making my own way (Birmingham by way of Beachy Head), I arrive at a destination already reached by others. For the idea of autonomous working groups within the factory, although little discussed, is not new either. In one form or another it is (as we should expect) part of our heritage from France. With his great emphasis upon the professional association and professional ethics, Durkheim is an obvious contributor in general terms to that tradition, but in the context of the factory it derives particularly from Louis Blanc's self-governing workshops in 1848—those more or less nationalized plants that, loosely regulated by the Government, were to drive the private workshops into bankruptcy. There the idea was potential rather than actual. It was actualized (I do not say for the first time) in the writing (and the life) of someone brought up in that post-1848 generation, Albert Thomas, the first Director of the International Labour Office at Geneva. As far back as 1924, he argued not for 'a limited influence on the general control' of the undertaking (or factory), but rather 'for complete management by the associated workers of each division in the undertaking which can technically be isolated from the latter's financial and commercial control'.[7] 'Free but responsible groups' within the undertaking, or factory: that was his ideal, whose standard was later kept aloft by his fellow-countryman, Hyacinthe Dubreuil.

Writing independently within the English tradition, H. A. Clegg, also, has anticipated me, even in the adaptation of the Guild Socialist 'collective contract' to the individual factory.[8] But he worked through to this position from political theory and from a careful review of the various forms of industrial democracy as actually tried out. When that review led him to reject workers' participation in management as a practicable form of industrial democracy, or self-government, he was driven to lowering his sights to the only level where self-government is even conceivable—the level of the self-governing,

[7] quoted in Dubreuil, ibid. For Durkheim, first consult *Professional Ethics and Civic Morals*, Routledge and Kegan Paul, 1958.

[8] H. A. Clegg, *A New Approach to Industrial Democracy*, Blackwell, 1960.

or autonomous, working group. I, on the other hand, have started from the facts of men's needs, and reach the idea of a Guild-in-miniature within the factory only after tracing the fate of those needs in factories as now organized, and asking myself what other arrangements would permit them to be better served. Different approaches have their peculiar merits (and defects). It is perhaps the merit of the social science approach that it can lay bare the motivational and normative reasons why 'social workshops', or 'collective contracts', *within* the factory are, in principle, important to the individual worker. At all events, I present the ideas here in order to suggest the only practicable way of meeting the higher root-needs of the ordinary workers, with all that that implies, both for them and the country as a whole. Thus, in intention, if not in actual achievement, I complement Clegg's work.

I do not, however, follow Clegg in the way in which the 'collective contract' should be regarded, which is important for the argument that follows in Part III. He concludes his review by agreeing that the ordinary worker cannot 'participate in management'. In the sense in which that phrase was always understood, the conclusion is no doubt true. I think myself, however, that deconcentration should be regarded as a special form of participation in management. In this I follow the older French tradition, as Thomas articulated it:

> 'These free but responsible groups, by doing away with the hierarchical subordination of the workers while at the same time maintaining contractually their technical inter-relation with the undertaking as a whole, result in a special form of participation by workers in management. But it should be noted that this type of participation does not represent a limited influence on the general control of the undertaking, but complete management by the associated workers of each division in the undertaking which can technically be isolated from the latter's financial and commercial control.'[9]

Dubreuil, too, regards this as 'a genuine form of management-sharing'. I think this conception, although different from the traditional English one, is tenable: workers participate or share in what must remain, in the ultimate, managerial authority.

Much more than the mere label is at stake here, although

[9] ibid.

what that is will not become apparent until Part III. But it may be as well to say now that I wish to keep the concept of 'participation in management' intact, and to be able to say that it has various applications, some of which are more crucial than others in providing the conditions for responsible behaviour in industry. This means that I still attach some importance to 'participation in management' even in the traditional sense. Limited as it has been and must be, too often an 'opaque sham' disguising manipulative control by management, it remains in principle of some value. By associating even a few of the workers with the strategic decisions of the factory, it may succeed in gratifying *their* higher needs. Certainly, it may enable the workers' representatives to underwrite the gratification of the lower needs of the many. For instance, participation, by yielding a supply of advance information about future developments, may help to serve the ordinary worker's need for safety. Because participation must be *by* the few, that does not mean that it cannot be *for* the many, in terms of needs-gratification.

If that is so, then, despite earlier disappointments and even disillusion, participation in the traditional sense is still worth striving for. There is another reason, too. If participation in the sense of deconcentration of powers to autonomous groups were set in hand, then participation in general control (the old sense of participation) might work much better than in the past. Deconcentration could be instituted only as a result of a sociological (or sociometric-type) analysis, in which the actual primary groups within the factory were identified and charted. It might well be that these autonomous, self-disciplining groups would prove to be far more effective foundations for a representative system than either individual 'atoms' or even departments or sections. At all events, we should keep open the door for further developments.

In short, I think of 'participation in management' as a continuum; at least as an arrangement to be sought at different levels. I entirely agree that the main goal must now become deconcentration to the primary groups, which, however, I regard as a special form of participation. On the other hand, participation even in the older sense still has point in terms of needs: the many needs of the few and even a few of the needs of the many.

CHAPTER ELEVEN

AUTONOMOUS GROUPS IN PRACTICE

So far I have allowed myself to be carried forward by the sweep of the argument, not pausing to ask whether autonomous groups are likely to work in every sense of the term. 'But will it *work*?' Our national suspicion of fancy schemes has to be allayed.

The evidence is now considerable that 'deconcentration' *can* work, and in such a variety of settings as to inspire confidence. It has worked in Labour Battalions in France during the 1914–18 War. These units undertook various 'dirty jobs', such as trench digging and moving ammunition. The various service corps said what had to be done (=took the 'strategic' decisions), but left it to the Labour Battalions to take responsibility and decide upon the most efficient method. It has worked in a textile mill in India. It has worked in the engineering industry in the United States in wartime. Owing to the shortage of managers and supervisors, a working group in one plant were left to manage themselves. Despite inferior physical conditions, that plant is said to have achieved a higher output than a sister plant managed in the normal way. It has worked in the engineering industry in the United States in peacetime. In a plant in Minnesota, the workers set their own work pace, the foremen giving few direct orders and becoming expediters rather than supervisors. Aided, presumably, by a guaranteed annual wage and by profit-sharing, they achieved a high level of productivity. Without benefit of profit-sharing (or representation on the board, etc.), it has worked in some French factories. There, under a collective work contract, workers agreed to produce goods at a certain price, which they then divided among themselves. They dispensed with all supervision. It has worked also in the toolroom of an English factory. Here groups of skilled workers were left to order their own materials; to define the method of manufacture, making their own work arrangements for each job; to estimate cost times and rates to be paid and so to price the job. An industrial consultant frankly expected an inefficient outcome to such a scheme—and was shocked to find that it worked.[1]

Above all it has worked in the North-West Durham coalfield. There, in the latter half of the 1950s, a changeover was taking place from traditional to newer mining methods resembling those used in manufacture. In the traditional method, single-place working, men take up positions on one small part of the coal face, which they work with a pick or pneumatic drill. The coal is carried away in tubs. In conventional longwall working, a long face (or longwall) is exposed, something like a hundred yards of it. It is worked by men in pairs, possibly using electric coal cutters. Behind them a conveyor carries off the coal to the tubs. The characteristic feature of this method is the high degree of division of labour, or role-segregation—one man, one job, in replacement of colliers in single-place working, who, self-selected and *self-supervising*, undertake a variety of jobs. It is the first stage of mechanization of the factory type. One man cuts, another clears, another does the stonework (shovelling the shot stone, erecting supports). But this work structure gives rise to acute problems of co-ordination and hence of *command*, external command, i.e. by management. External command, however, is not practicable in underground conditions, and therefore it is not surprising if some of the results of early mechanization were disappointing. At all events, there was a move to return to all-roundness, as against high role-segregation, and to self-supervision (i.e. to autonomy).

So there came about a transition to composite longwall working. In this a man was treated once again as a face-worker, not as a cutter, filler, stoneman, or occupier of some other specialized role. In principle, the workers were interchangeable at need. Each was regarded as making a contribution of equivalent value; accordingly, the rewards (so much per shift

[1] C. H. Northcott, *Economic Journal*, March, 1924, as quoted in J. A. C. Brown, op. cit., p. 235; A. K. Rice, *Productivity and Social Organization: the Ahmedabad Experiment*, Tavistock, 1958; R. P. Lynton, op. cit., pp. 127, 148–9, 152; Fred H. Blum, *Toward a Democratic Work Process*, Harper, 1953; G. D. H. Cole, *An Introduction to Trade Unionism*, Allen and Unwin, 1953, p. 232; James J. Gillespie, *Free Expression in Industry*, The Pilot Press, 1948.

plus an incentive bonus on output) were equally divided. To a substantial degree, the members of the primary work-group of some forty to fifty were self-selected. Not entirely so; to make the fullest use of high-capacity machines and to achieve a balance of skills, including leadership ability, management, in consultation with the lodge (or union), determined the broad role-structure of the work-group and the seam to be worked. But the allocation of persons to roles, rotation of shifts for the work-force of forty to fifty miners, the day-by-day management of work problems—all this was left to the group. As long as the coal face lasted, some two years, they ran the job themselves, an autonomous, self-disciplining group, who were, at the end of the period, still growing in their capacity to make adaptations to changing circumstances and to satisfy the needs of their members.

But, ask the canny ones, what were the output results? The general results were extremely encouraging. Under conventional longwall working, each little team (cuttermen, fillers, etc.) had gone about its own business with little thought for the others at hand. Thus a cutterman might 'crop' (leave a part of the ground uncut, his machine having risen a little): the filler would have to remove it with a pick. Under composite working, the standard of workmanship was 'quite evidently' higher. Here the workers took thought not only for the others immediately to hand but also for those coming on the next shift. For instance, men who on a particular shift had completed their own task carried on working, so that the next shift would have a bit in hand to meet unexpected difficulties. Under conventional working, the relations between cuttermen, fillers (of the shot coal) and pullers (who move the conveyor and build up the advancing coal face) had been to some extent competitive; under the composite method, they had a common goal. The composite method gave men more variety in their roles and in the shifts worked. The frustration of the fillers and stonemen was noticeably reduced. Absences from sickness and accidents generally were halved; absences where no reasons were forthcoming declined dramatically, and virtually disappeared. Production was up to schedule and sometimes ahead of it. Productivity increased from an *overall* 3.5 tons per man-shift (at the face) to 5.3 tons; in the judgement of the hard-headed researchers from the Tavistock Institute of Human Relations, led by E. L. Trist, who conducted this masterly research,[2] the men were producing 95% of their potential.

Nor was that all. Maintaining the *cycle* of production now became more of a challenge, but in general day-to-day pressure on management was reduced. One official could be dispensed with; the undermanager could turn his attention to other things. Less time had to be devoted to immediate issues; arguments about the price-list, for instance, fell in one quarter from 170 to 7. More time could be devoted by management to safety and other matters. Generally, management could 'forget about' that particular seam and so was left free to think creatively about the problems of the colliery as a whole. For, of course, 'some of the managing had been taken over by the primary group—the part appropriate to its own task'. In the usage I prefer, the workers by participating in management, leave the managers free for a more creative managerial role, problem-solving rather than merely executive. Thus along every dimension, economic (or financial) as well as human, 'responsible autonomy' worked. In the language of the canny ones, it 'paid dividends', than which, surely, there can be no higher praise.

Other examples could be adduced (for instance, from a mine in the Donbass area of the Soviet Union, where, apparently in the mid-fifties, a similar change from conventional to composite longwall working is reported to have achieved a remarkable increase in productivity).[3] But a multiplication of examples would serve little purpose. The point of all of them other than the Durham coalfield case is *not* that they provide 'proof' of the position reached by another route. Rather they are meant to illustrate that what seems to be the only way of meeting the higher root-needs of ordinary workers in factories *is* practicable in many different settings and cultures, and so cannot be patronizingly dismissed as another reformist dream.

The Durham case, on the other hand, takes us as far as the social sciences can in establishing a socially important proposition. The research team from the Tavistock Institute was a

[2] E. K. Trist, G. W. Higgin, H. Murray, A. B. Pollock, *Organizational Choice*, Tavistock, 1963.

[3] ibid., pp. 281–2.

distinguished one. The period they actually surveyed covered some three years (1955–58), but altogether they devoted some ten years to it. They were able to take the same seam, in the same pit, in the same general geological and mining conditions, where the same cutting methods were in use; the same neighbourhood and the same type of man; all the ostensibly relevant factors, in short, were held constant other than the two contrasting longwall methods. The results, therefore, command a very high degree of confidence.

These results accord very well with the drift of the argument so far. The deconcentration of power to the primary group gave some forty or fifty men, not merely a few representatives, the chance to gratify, if not completely then much more fully, their higher needs. Though 'weighted' for special skills, the group was to a very substantial degree self-selected; this alone would have helped the service of the affiliative need, and interaction in a comparatively happy atmosphere would have completed what substantial self-selection began. The need for esteem (or recognition) would have been served by the interchangeability of tasks, and by the sense of pulling one's weight for the team. Correspondingly, self-fulfilment (or achievement) would have been satisfied in some degree, thanks in part to the greater variety as between both tasks and shifts, and above all to the obligation (no burden because self-imposed) to take each day a fairly wide range of managerial-type decisions. Frustration would thus be reduced, and so the various behavioural responses to it. Voluntary absenteeism, for example, dropped off sharply, most noticeably among the fillers and stonemen (whose frustration had been observed by the researchers) but not, apparently, among them alone. In turn the men's dispositions to respond to others would come to be modified, and so, in due course, their individual attitudes and primary-group norms. Out of that complex interplay and adjustment would have come the remarkable increase in productivity.

Thus 'responsible autonomy', as Trist calls it, is a way of enabling men's higher needs to be more fully gratified, and, if the earlier argument is sound, it is the *only* way. This development would have implications for the characters of the workers. A hint that the expected character changes were beginning to take place is provided by Trist and his associates. Under the composite longwall method, workers began to think rather more of the next man, and even of the men on the next shift. Instead of regarding their fellow-workers as (in some degree) rivals, they began to co-operate with them more fully. Above all, they helped men who were not even present—those due on the next shift—by carrying on even after their own particular task had been completed. That is immensely significant: it is nothing less than a glimmering of the sense of civic obligation. Appealed to face-to-face, anyone can be helpful; it requires an effort of the moral imagination to put oneself out for somebody who is 'faceless', which is what the discharge of civic obligation (for 'the public' or 'the community') demands. Obviously, that was only a beginning; the workers knew the men on the next shift and were indeed part of the same primary group. But that is just the point: the loyalty area had been extended, the ambit of men's altruism widened. If the work structures in ten thousand plants enabled us to think, day after day, of the man on the next shift (or some equivalent extension of *self*), would anyone doubt that a concern for the 'nameless' others would increasingly become a part of the characters of the workers?

What Trist and his associates have done, in fact, is to give as near a scientific demonstration as we can hope to have of the French sociologist, Durkheim's claims about the moral significance of the division of labour. Durkheim argued that the weakening of the ties between individual and family (soil, traditions, customs) that is the consequence of geographical mobility in the new industrial order tends to a debasement of morality. Men no longer feel obligated, no longer feel the 'salutary pressure' of society to moderate their egoism and make them moral beings. But what does 'moral' mean here? Everything, anything, that makes a man take account of other men is moral; everything, anything, that requires a man to regulate his conduct through something other than the striving of his ego is moral. Morality is as solid as these ties are numerous and strong. Now the division of labour makes man aware of his dependence on society, while at the same time checking and restraining him. Thus the division of labour is the chief source of social solidarity and so at the same time the foundation of the moral order. It is this that gives moral value to the division of labour.[4]

Durkheim's mood is indicative; we should have to say now that such moral value is conditional upon our deliberately creating the appropriate work structure. It is in the 'free but responsible' work groups that morality, or a wider concern for the public good, can grow—and only there. Durkheim saw in the division of labour the root of an 'occupational morality'. That is what it can produce, given the right structure; at the same time it can yield more than that. The choice is ours.

It may, however, be objected: what are the conditions of, and so limitations upon, choice? Are there no dangers in the collective contract? Historically, it has not always satisfied the workers; in the British motor car industry before the 1939–45 War, for instance, the rest of the 'gang' felt that only the charge hands and the leading hands did well financially out of it.[5] In the nineteenth century, exploitation of the gang by the gang leader did occur.[6] I cannot believe, however, that the possibility of exploitation still presents a serious obstacle to the application of the idea, since appropriate provisions could easily be incorporated in the contract itself, which would also be 'policed' by the full-time union officials.

The general problem, however, cannot be summarily dismissed but has to be accepted as formidable. How, H. A. Clegg has asked, can the collective contract (responsible autonomy) 'be applied to industries where the natural groupings of men at work are very different from those at the coalface, as in road transport at one extreme, or in a large belt-production system at the other?'[7] Taking particular cases before the general proposition, I am inclined to think that the road transport example, apparently so conclusive, is less so when scrutinized. If it is 'bus services we have in mind, I see no reason why general decisions about shift working, crew make-up and the like should not be taken on a group basis at the depot. Workers may be no less a social group simply because they go out in pairs so long as they can return fairly easily to some convenient

[4] *The Division of Labour in Society*, Free Press, 1947 (translated by George Simpson).

[5] Seymour Melman, op. cit., p. 34.

[6] H. A. Clegg, *A New Approach to Industrial Democracy*, Blackwell, 1960, p. 125.

[7] Ibid., pp. 124–5.

centre to act in concert. This conception agrees with Faris's modification of the original notion of *primary group*, where the face-to-face attribute postulated by Cooley gives place to a psychological identity, such that members of an affectionate family, although widely separated in space, may yet 'belong'.[8] Everything would seem to depend upon the evidence in each case; accordingly, the issue is one for further inquiry.

On the other hand, if by 'road transport' we mean road haulage, then it might prove useful to distinguish between long-distance runs and short hauls, including hauls between factories. In the American motor car industry, for example, Leonard Sayles observed that the in-plant and between-plant truckers (lorry drivers carrying car bodies) developed 'a real *esprit de corps*', which under some other name is surely one of the distinguishing features of a social group. That spirit arose partly in virtue of the truckers' evident skill and stamina but in part precisely because of their very mobility, which was seen to contribute so much to the success of the enterprise. Sayles made another observation that has some bearing upon the question; he found that in many American industrial groups, including the truckers, size was not limited by the ability of the individual to respond to others in day-to-day interaction.[9] As for the longer hauls, very much depends upon *how long* and upon the turnround. London to Edinburgh (400 miles) is one thing; London to Brighton (50 miles) and even London to Bristol (100 miles) quite another. Particularly with the opening of the motorways, it should not be beyond the wit of man, for the shorter long-hauls, to find a time and place for the common determination (within the agreed range) of driving and other work conditions. If so, the question would revolve (granted the turnround) upon the ratio of the different types of 'runs', although even then the actual pattern might be susceptible of some modification if autonomous-group decision-making were considered of sufficient importance.

The attainment of responsible autonomy in a large belt-production system is undeniably extremely difficult. Here both the *a priori* probabilities and actual evidence are clear and consistent: for short assembly lines as well as long, this tech-

[8] See ch. Five, n. 3 and text.

[9] op. cit., pp. 23 and 158.

nology does stifle interaction among workers.[10] That, however, does not dispose of the matter completely, for it fails to take into account at least one relevant factor other than technology: the undisputed tendencies of the assembly line may be counteracted in some degree by appropriate supervision. As Zaleznik judged from his study (mid-1950s) of a machine shop in a small instrument-manufacturing company in the United States—

> 'Where technological organization of work acts as a constraint on a group because of severe limitations on interaction, the burden for developing an effective group falls heavily upon supervisors. They become the centres of communication and must exercise a high degree of skill to relate workers to each other where in other technical settings workers can develop their relationships on their own."[11]

That was a judgement formed in terms of a short assembly line, but it held good, according to Zaleznik, for longer ones as well. The conclusion seems to be that there are more factors (or variables) than one to be considered, and these need not pull in the same direction but may, on the contrary, be set in fruitful opposition. If that, judging by the unhappy labour relations attaching to assembly-line production, is, ostensibly, not what actually happens, it does not mean that we could not give a better account of ourselves if we began thinking seriously about the broad social ends that industry ought to be attempting to achieve.

Of course it would be foolish to pretend that assembly-line technology is other than a tall, spiky obstacle in my path; I might also have to concede road transport, or some sections of it, as a special case. But that leaves me open to the objection: how general is special? Of course, I do not know: we lack basic information such as sociometric-type maps of British industry (charting relationships and interactions) in terms of the several technologies. But some suggestions can be made, especially in relation to H. A. Clegg's proposition about 'natural groupings'. I suspect that factory groupings are 'natural' only to industrial engineers and planners, who ought to be allowed the first but not the last word in matters that

[10] A. Zaleznik, *Worker Satisfaction and Development*, Harvard University Graduate School of Business Administration, 1956, pp. 120–5.

[11] Ibid., p. 122.

penetrate, if the general argument is sound, deep into the soil of our national life. At all events, we must cease to believe, against the evidence, that technology wholly determines work organization, and that this in turn wholly determines (the relevant) social structure. If the industrial engineer is given his head and technology has therefore to be taken as given, the way in which those who do the job are related to one another (i.e. the work organization) is not so; an area of choice remains, smaller than we would wish but larger than we often fear. This, as we saw, is the point of Eric Trist's book—*Organizational Choice*. And it finds support, as a fairly general proposition *not* confined to coal-mining, in the work of Robert Blauner for the United States.[12]

That even a work organization apparently quite unfavourable to group formation may not prove to be so stands out clearly from Zaleznik's researches in that American machine shop of fourteen workers and their foreman. At the outset the shop seemed to Zaleznik to hold out almost no hope for any integrated social grouping. The work flow derived from the technology outlined a pattern of interaction among the machinists and operators that seemed to embrace only *worker:foreman*. Similarly, spatial relations (layout and job positions) seemed inimical to group formation. The scene appeared to be set for a 'dust-heap' of unrelated individuals or for highly-divisive cliques. In fact, the workers produced a fairly elaborate social structure: an informal work-group linked to two 'social' groups (card-playing and conversation), with common membership. Admittedly, the extent to which the informal work-group, which constituted only one part of the whole shop, could be built upon for autonomous decision-making would have to be investigated further. Yet its appearance in such unfavourable circumstances is a tribute to the strength of the underlying forces, and suggests that we should give very much more thought to the factors that encourage or hinder such social formations and to the possible use of these for responsible autonomy. Accordingly, I tentatively suggest that neither *technology: work organization* nor *work organization: (relevant) social structure* necessarily entails a 'one-to-one' relationship, but that a margin of 'tolerance' exists, already sufficient to permit some

[12] *Alienation and Freedom*, University of Chicago Press, 1964.

freedom of manoeuvre. This might even be extended appreciably if we kept the industrial engineer in his place as one expert among many, and asked ourselves whether fundamental social decisions ought not to be put rather in the hands of those who are qualified to make them.

What, however, of future trends? Are these ruinous of my line of thought? I will make the test more severe by confining myself to the first relationship and by banishing the margin of tolerance. Following Robert Blauner throughout, I distinguish four types of technology. By 'technology' is here meant the combination of certain physical objects and technical operations, both manual and machine, in the production of goods and services: fundamentally, it denotes the machine system, the technical knowledge and mechanical skills used in industrial production. Craft technology, exemplified by printing, needs no introduction; nor simple mechanization, as in light assembly. Assembly-line production is also familiar. Continuous-process technology, however, still has an aura of freshness. A species of automation, it is exemplified by oil refining. For arguments' sake suppose now that simple machine technologies make for informal social groups and a high degree of cohesion but that assembly-line production subverts them and hinders cohesion. Continuous-process production, too, stands as an even more patent obstacle to the development of social groups since, by drastically reducing the number of men required, it tends to dispense with the raw material. The men are also much changed in character: white-collared, not blue-collared, spending their time monitoring instruments on a panel or maintaining the machinery when it stops being as automatic as was intended. Here group formation withers at the roots; indeed, the whole industrial problem tends to be made less difficult by the resulting 'Balkanization' of industry, factories becoming smaller in absolute size and, within their walls, opportunities for small team work and potential loyalty and identification between worker and firm.[13]

The question, then, becomes: does industrial advance consist in a progression from the simpler technologies to technologies of these two kinds (and perhaps others of which we are as yet but dimly aware)? It is tempting to think of the

[13] Ibid.

development of technology as unilinear, i.e. from craft technology to simple mechanization and so to the assembly-line, reaching a sort of pinnacle in continuous-process. Such a progression can be partially observed in some industries: glass-making advances from a craft to mass-production; shoemaking from craft to mechanization and even the assembly-line. And in a very broad way our industrial history is a history of such advances. Yet that is so only in a very broad way. The development is obviously uneven. Why is that so? 'Culture lag' might be part of the explanation, but more fundamentally we should look at the very determinants of technology. Granted the economic and engineering resources of the firm, the determinants are the general level of mechanical and technical knowledge, and, perhaps above all, the nature of the product itself. If the product is not standardized but unique, that rules out or limits the use of complex machine production; one might have batch production. Only products of a certain composition (fluid and homogeneous, like oil) lend themselves to automated continuous-process technology. Thus the nature of the product sets some limit to the application of the advanced methods. Economic questions of another kind obtrude: what is the relevant cost structure? Is the industry growing?

Simply by bringing into focus a few of the factors, we see the very great complexity of the issue: even some reversal of current trends should not be completely ruled out. Certainly, it is impossible to be sure what 'combination' of technologies to expect in the next half century, allowing for time-lags as well as for new developments, military and political no less than technical and economic. Yet we must not falter in coming to public decisions simply because we cannot forecast precisely, nor remain inert simply because we do not fully understand. It is not merely that indecision is a kind of decision, shaping the future (a mosaic formed, in part, from innumerable current decisions), but that withdrawal from the great challenges of public life leads into the cave where private cults flourish and only the shadows are real. Public life is the life of decision to strive for goals only dimly perceived and only partially within our grasp by means only imperfectly understood. We read the great literature, imaginative as well as technical; we reflect quietly; we dispute vigorously; we do not ignore difficulties—

but neither do we expire under the weight of them. Not all social problems are soluble, but they are not all insoluble either. In the end, we *decide.* In the present context, having already used thought as a prelude to action, we know that in *choosing*, for example, a method of work organization, we are *choosing* very much more in terms of men's needs, and ultimately influencing strikes, absenteeism and the like, and even productivity. Even the highest affairs of State, as with incomes policy and 'guidelines', are touched by it, and could be influenced still more. It is indeed strange to reflect that in willing a method of work organization, we are having some influence upon ostensibly remote issues of high policy. But it is true: let us apply that knowledge where we can and as best we may, now. The difficulties we can take in our stride, tomorrow.

PART III

Towards civic virtue

CHAPTER TWELVE

EDUCATION FOR CIVIC VIRTUE

The next task, then, is to discuss how an occupational morality might be turned into a civic morality. We have to extend the workers' concern for the man at the next bench and on the next shift to a concern for the community as a whole, so that necessary national policies come to be accepted and implemented. It *is* a long day's march, and some have despaired of reaching the destination. The English sociologist, T. H. Marshall, commenting upon a trade union leader's plea, in 1948, for a full contribution from both sides of industry to the national economy and world recovery, objected:

> 'But the national community is too large and remote to command this kind of loyalty and to make of it a continual driving force. That is why many people think that the solution of our problem lies in the development of more limited loyalties, to the local community and especially to the working group. In this latter form industrial citizenship, devolving its obligations down to the basic units of production, might supply some of the vigour that citizenship in general appears to lack.'[1]

The concrete suggestion is excellent as far as it goes, yet the perspective is surely distorted. If 'industrial citizenship' were all we could hope for, our situation would be irredeemable: we could never look forward to a time when the local unions would, for example, check earnings-drift or exercise any other form of self-discipline. But the implied antithesis, based on a static sociology, is surely false. A vigorous industrial citizenship maintained over a considerable period would tend to change both local union norms and the character (attitudes) of local union members. The human material would no longer be the same. From a base in the primary work-group, therefore, it

[1] 'Citizenship and Social Class' in *Sociology at the Crossroads*, Heinemann, 1963, p. 124.

ought to be possible to build upwards until the right ordering of the workers' several loyalties (me and mine; those working beside me; the next shift; the colliery, plant or office; the firm; my next-door neighbour; my town . . . my country) becomes, through *learning*, settled habit, i.e. embedded in character.

Such a process would not, of course, take place of its own accord: free but responsible groups at work are only the indispensable beginning. To achieve more (and nothing less than 'more' will do), the process must be influenced at every stage by education, using the term in a very broad sense to include not only socialization but 'the deeper language of example and the more living instruction of visible circumstance', as the English historian, John Morley, wrote in the rather different though not unrelated context of Rousseau's essay on education, *Émile*.[2]

For education as socialization, we have to revive and adapt Plato's great conception of a State systematically training its citizens to virtue, although we should have to mean *all* citizens, not a few of them, as Plato himself intended in his earlier formulation. By 'virtue', of course, the Greeks did not mean 'moral virtue', but the highest excellence or perfection of everything, of which moral virtue is but a particular species.[3] For the purpose in hand, we might say, somewhat loosely, that civic virtue is the highest excellence of citizenship.

This training would begin at school. In his late work, the *Laws*, Plato visualized such education in boyhood as to inspire—

> 'the recipient with a passionate and ardent desire to become a perfect citizen, knowing both how to wield and how to submit to righteous rule.'[4]

That is an ideal, but we can fairly expect a system of education in which the right ordering of our several loyalties is as systematically discussed as it is now systematically neglected. This implies that in schools, colleges and universities, the present emphasis on the transmission of knowledge, techniques and skills should give way to an emphasis on values. Of course, the antithesis is too sharp: values are to some extent embodied or

[2] Everyman's Library, ed. by Ernest Rhys, 1948 ed., p. viii.

[3] Werner Jaeger, *Aristotle*, Oxford Paperbacks, 1962, p. 417.

[4] Everyman's Library, ed. by A. E. Taylor, p. 21 (643D–644B).

implied in what we now transmit. But these values, when brought to light, may not be appropriate to civic virtue; indeed, the very concentration upon techniques and skills, with its implicit bias towards 'getting on' at all costs, trampling over anyone who stands in the way, may well work against it. In any case, the values need to be isolated, identified, interpreted in the light of contemporary conditions and issues, discussed, refined, *consciously* transmitted.

In Durkheim's more elaborate formulation, we should seek to inculcate not only particular virtues through particular duties but also a general aptitude for morality in the sense of a permanent bent towards concern for the interest of others collectively conceived, i.e. for the public good.[5] In accordance with that conception of morality, Durkheim saw moral education as comprising three parts: the inculcation of the spirit of discipline; attachment to social groups; and autonomy, or self-determination. Discipline means obeying the norms prescribing our conduct in specific situations, whether person-to-person or person-to-property. The function of this element in morality is to eliminate arbitrariness from man's behaviour, and by that token to induce regularities. The end-product should be an attitude or disposition of restraint, not as some faint-hearted resignation or wringing of hands but as recognition that each of us is bound by the physical and social environment. It is to be the restraint of realistic objectives.[6]

Discipline, however, is but a formal property of a moral education; what should be its substance? For the answer to that question we have to examine the nature of those objectives about which man is enjoined to be realistic. Such objectives will be on behalf either of the individual himself or of some entity other than himself, such as a social group or association. By common consent moral action has to do with objectives of the second kind; a moral objective is one whose referent is some collectivity or other, or, at a higher level of abstraction, the public. Moral action is action for the public good. Thus the area of the moral begins where the area of the social begins, and morality links man to objectives that extend beyond his

[5] *Education and Sociology* (introduction by Sherwood D. Fox), Free Press, 1956, pp. 41 and 76.

[6] *Moral Education* (ed. by Everett K. Wilson), Free Press, 1961, Part I.

immediate circle, or, in the Keynesian phrase, that widens the ambit of his altruism. It is not a question, however, of total renunciation, of utter self-denial, but of striking the sort of creative balance that permits a man to grow as a human being. In terms of content, then, moral education would implant this feeling for the public good.

In its third aspect, moral education would train the understanding, so that men assented freely, not followed blindly, the customary standards of morality (in the sense indicated, not its reduction to the level of the merely sexual). Durkheim here intends to produce a self-determined man. This is of crucial importance because it implicitly dispels the understandable but mistaken impression that Durkheim's moral education would really prepare the individual for some murmuring immolation at the altar of the Group. The true aim is, in the end, the rounded development of the individual person, and as for achievement, I hold that, far from mutilating man, it would work towards that release from unbridled self which permits entry into the realm of one kind of freedom. In fashioning what he imagines to be 'a secular morality', the brilliant Jew of our epoch echoes, not for the first time, the thoughts if not quite the words of that other Jew of long ago. When that convergence is understood, one ought not to be surprised if one's unconscious prompter brings swiftly to the surface the words of the distinguished educationist, Sir Fred Clarke—

> 'It may be that the most essentially religious thing in us is that by virtue of which we cohere as a society, and that there is the heart of Education's business.'[7]

'Education's business' cannot, of course, be carried on by schools, colleges and universities alone. What these begin, the adult education system must continue if not complete (if only because the task will never be completed). We must abandon the curious notion that somehow education comes to an end in early manhood, and recognize instead that it is coterminous with life itself. But adult education, too, would have to change its priorities, and concern itself far more with values, discovering a sense of social purpose of a different kind. This social purpose, however, would not be fully discharged by

[7] *Education and Social Change*, Sheldon Press, 1940.

continuation-work alone. It would be important to try to reach the existing parents, otherwise within the family, for most social scientists the agency of socialization *par excellence*, the older culture would be perpetuated, which would, of course put children under cross-pressure and make the whole task of reclamation that much more difficult. We must envisage a simultaneous operation on several fronts, not the single frontal attack of traditional reforms.

For different reasons, this emphasis upon the State's training citizens to virtue will cause some disquiet and even alarm. Some will wonder whether the State would not brand its citizens too well. In the hands of that eighteenth-century Platonist, Jean Jacques Rousseau, the Greek emphasis comes out as an injunction to the State to put upon its members the national stamp and 'so direct their opinions and their tastes, that they are patriots by inclination, by passion, and by necessity'.[8] It must surely be possible, however, to stop short of such an extreme 'education' while yet inculcating in our citizenry that settled habit of concern for others which, at its highest, is civic virtue. Nor should it be overlooked that to speak of 'the State's training citizens to virtue' is merely a convenient shorthand. The actual work would be in the hands of our educationists, given their head on a simple basis of agreement about the right emphasis in education—that, at least, it should be as much about the meaning of existence, man's place in the world and his relations with his fellows in society as about the transfer of neat lumps of knowledge in coloured plastic bags and the training of intelligence. In short, they would be agreed that education ought mainly to mean the training of the moral sympathies as well as of the intelligence; the rest is secondary. The State's role would be that of energizer, co-ordinator, financial provider.

Even that may not be entirely acceptable to those who put their faith in other agencies of socialization, notably the Church. The characteristic Greek conception of the function of the State—the production of virtue—was, of course, formulated some four centuries before the star rose in the East. Evidently, the Church can make a major contribution, some of its priests and ministers reverting to the role of simple teachers, in the

[8] Constitution for Poland.

highways and by-ways as well as in their own halls and vestries, and even within the adult education framework. Yet, once again, the onus must be on the State, for at least four reasons. Only the State can initiate, supply the funds and co-ordinate the effort on the scale required. The educational channels in the narrower sense have been largely secularized. Education for civic virtue implies, for the best results at least, a particular organization or method—that which Aristotle recommended for the education of the young.[9] Discussing the formation, including the improvement of national character, as a prerequisite of constitutional improvement, he taught that education ought to be one and the same, which meant that both the running of it and the pursuit of it ought to be public, i.e. *by* the State (it was actually private in Greece) and *in* common. As the Oxford classicist, W. L. Newman, put it: 'those who are to work together as members of the same State should be educated in the same way and educated together'.[10] This is not simply to have common studies but above all so that 'a public aim will be impressed on the education of the individual'. Since the individual is part of a community, the fact should be recognized in the way education is organized; boys and girls, in the words of the Conservative philosopher-statesman, Arthur Balfour, should be given a sense of being part of 'an enduring "Whole" '. If an education in common is possible at all, only the State can now arrange it. Finally, what the State, through its educationists, does not do, agencies other than itself and the Church, will assume, even if unintentionally. If the State stands back, others in effect step in. The State's aloofness or impartiality becomes the partiality of the hucksters, the wheeler-dealers, the 'front' organizers and the smooth insinuators. For the State to refrain is to let others prevail. In short, the State has to assume major, although not exclusive, responsibility for teaching some of the basic values of the community, not excluding new values or re-interpretations of old ones. As Durkheim saw, the State must persevere in calling the individual to a moral way of life.[11]

[9] *Politics*, Book VIII.

[10] W. L. Newman, *The Politics of Aristotle*, the Clarendon Press, 1887, vol. I, pp. 353–4.

[11] *Professional Ethics and Civic Morals*, Routledge and Kegan Paul, 1958, p. 69.

The right type of education in the sense of socialization would have to be supplemented by education through the deeper language of example and practice. Here we must again grasp at old truths. The Greeks well understood that a constitution ('the ordering of the magistracies [offices] of a State, and especially of the supreme authority')[12] has influence for good or evil. Each constitution embodies an ethos, which makes itself felt in all the relations of life. Each constitutional form has a moulding influence on virtue, so that in an aristocracy the good citizen is one thing, in a democracy quite another. Each constitution embodies a scheme of life, and tends, as a latent or unintended consequence, to bring those living under it into harmony with its particular scheme. One aspect of this comes out in Aristotle's own example: if the constitution provides that the highest offices in the State shall be purchaseable or confined to wealthy men, it will by that very emphasis tend to inspire a respect for wealth in its citizens. Here we see the fundamental reason why Greek writers were not content, in the final analysis, to classify constitutions in terms of numbers, i.e. according to whether supreme authority was in the hands of one person, the few or the many. If constitutions have ethical force, they should also be classified according to their ethical consequences. The very fact that it is the classification by numbers that has survived into modern political science is significant; it suggests how far the other conception has lost ground and indeed almost disappeared from view (and also how narrow political science has become).

As recently as the Victorians, the ethical influence of institutions was well understood. W. L. Newman discussed a special aspect of it under the heading of the impact of law. This, he taught at Balliol College, Oxford, does far more than protect property and person; it tends, incidentally, 'to develop a type of character (ethos), or at least to modify in some degree the predominant motives of action'. Thus, primogeniture, monogamy and other laws or social practices exercise 'powerful influences on character'; they not only enforce certain outward acts, but they create dispositions'.[13] That is the voice of the modern social scientist, and, replacing 'character' by 'person-

[12] Newman, p. 243.
[13] ibid., p. 76.

ality', the terminology too. But the great articulation of the Greek tradition is in John Stuart Mill:

> 'The business of life is an essential part of the practical education of a people; without which, book and school instruction, though most necessary and salutary, does not suffice to qualify them for conduct, and for the adaptation of means to ends. Instruction is only one of the desiderata of mental improvement; another, almost as indispensable, is a vigorous exercise of the active energies; labour, contrivance, judgment, self-control: and the natural stimulus to these is the difficulties of life.'

Now since these difficulties cannot be done away with, only diminished, the quality of practical judgment in the affairs of life should be cultivated not merely in a select few but in all. Since that cultivation should be more varied and complete than most people are able to find in the narrow sphere of their merely individual interests, we should look outside:

> 'A people among whom there is no habit of spontaneous action for a collective interest—who look habitually to their government to command or prompt them in all matters of joint concern—who expect to have everything done for them, except what can be made an affair of mere habit and routine—have their faculties only half developed; their education is defective in one of its most important branches. Not only is the cultivation of the active faculties by exercise, diffused through the whole community, in itself one of the most valuable of national possessions: it is rendered, not less, but more, necessary, by the fact that a high degree of that indispensable culture is systematically kept up in the chiefs and functionaries of the state. There cannot be a combination of circumstances more dangerous to human welfare, than that in which intelligence and talent are maintained at a high standard within a governing corporation, but starved and discouraged outside the pale. Such a system, more completely than any other, embodies the idea of despotism, by arming with intellectual superiority as an additional weapon, those who have already the legal power. It approaches as nearly as the organic difference between human beings and other animals admits to the government of sheep by their shepherd, without anything like so strong an interest as the shepherd has in the thriving condition of the flock. The only security against political slavery, is the check maintained over governors, by the diffusion of intelligence, activity, and public spirit among the governed.'

As life gets easier, Mill thought, there would be great difficulty in keeping up these high standards. Accordingly, he added this warning—

> 'It is therefore of supreme importance that all classes of the community, down to the lowest, should have much to do for themselves; that as great a demand should be made upon their intelligence and virtue as it is in any respect equal to; that the government should not only leave as much as possible to their own faculties the conduct of whatever concerns themselves alone, but should suffer them, or rather encourage them, to manage as many as possible of their joint concerns by voluntary co-operation: since the discussion and management of collective interests is the great school of that public spirit, and the great source of that intelligence of public affairs, which are always regarded as the distinctive character of the public of free countries.'[14]

Of course, since Mill wrote in 1848, we have learned by bitter experience that the scope for voluntary enterprise is smaller than he then thought. The 'management of collective interests' is now achieved through a different balance or combination of social forces. But it remains true that the 'management of collective interests' in some form *is* the great school of the public spirit, or, in the language here used, of civic virtue.

A generation later this truth was well expressed in different terms. Some author had written to the effect that whereas man tames and educates some lower animals, he has no higher animal to educate him. A reviewer, classical scholar perhaps or one of the new sociologists, agreed that the remark was strictly true but commented:

> 'yet in all organized communities the individual man is submitted to a superior control—namely, that of society and of social, as distinct from individual, ends of action; and the education of man in his individual character by man in his corporate or political character is really a far greater and more wonderful thing than the development of the half-human intelligence, wonderful as that is, of a well-bred and well-trained dog.'[15]

In other words, education for civic virtue is really self-

[14] *Principles of Political Economy*, John W. Parker, London 1848, vol. II, Book V, pp. 513–15.

[15] Quoted in Newman, p. 288.

education. As Ernest Barker, a great teacher, put it: 'Men educate themselves for citizenship by doing as well as learning'.[16] By 'doing' he meant being a member of voluntary bodies: clubs, university tutorial classes, community associations, churches, chapels and village institutes. This, he taught, is the practice of citizenship, which is not just voting or attending political meetings; it 'is saying good and considered words into the middle, in any group, and on any occasion when it is possible'. That, appropriately, is the voice of the translator of Aristotle. I would merely stress, from the perspective of social psychology, that to *do* is also to *learn*. That is what his Greek masters taught; and the twentieth-century social psychologist can only agree.

[16] Ernest Barker, 'The Citizen's Choice', in *The Teaching of Politics*, Oxford University Press, 1937, pp. 158–60.

CHAPTER THIRTEEN

INSTITUTIONS FOR CIVIC VIRTUE

If institutions have an ethical influence, then by shaping these along certain lines it ought to be possible to induce certain ethical tendencies: *this* sort of institution, *that* sort of virtue. Our concern here is not with those specific virtues (temperance, courage) that Greek writers drew either from Greek experience or from introspection. In practice, no doubt, statesmen and their political-scientist advisers would not be able to confine themselves to the production of one type of virtue. But what we might regard as the virtue of the citizen's function—the due discharge of civic obligation—is of such overriding importance whatever the circumstances that the present argument need not look beyond it.

How, then, may we so adapt our political institutions as to induce a tendency towards civic virtue? The work of Trist and his associates at the Durham coalfield provides the key to this question as well as a bridge to classical Greek practice. The area of men's loyalty (the ambit of their altruism) began to widen when one institutional pattern (the conventional longwall work-structure) was replaced by another (the composite). The essence of this new pattern embodying the autonomous group was that it provided a kind of participation in management. Thus the tendency to take others into account—the germ of civic virtue—arose, in this instance, out of regular participation in decision-making.

Now this is what theory would lead us to expect. Participation is a way (*the* way) of gratifying men's needs, especially the higher ones, and the gratification of men's needs has implications for both behaviour and character. Yet the Durham experience can be taken only as a clue or strong hint: we have to look elsewhere for further enlightenment. I can think of nowhere better than the Athens of the fifth and fourth centuries, B.C.

As a type, the Greek city-state, of which Athens is commonly thought to be the highest embodiment, developed during the age of Homer; 800 B.C. is a useful date for getting one's bearings.[1] Characteristically, a city-state was a town (or urban nucleus), usually walled, set in a rural hinterland that was politically united to it. Some districts were fragmented: Boeotia, for instance, was divided at one period into ten, at another period into twenty, political units. In Athens, however, as a result of a long process of expansion ending in the eighth century, town and district (Attica) were politically one. By the time Plato was born in the late fifth century, perhaps three out of five of the total population (as distinct from citizens) lived in the 'built up' area. Every City-State was small, even tiny, by modern standards, both in area and population. Geographically the largest, Sparta (with Laconia and Messenia) had only 3300 square miles—much less than half (four-tenths) the size of Wales. Athens and Boeotia were about a third as extensive. Just before Plato was born Athens had a population variously estimated at 215–300,000.[2]

The city-states were (in their hey-day) self-governing but within them the distribution of political power varied widely. At first power was everywhere narrowly confined to one pair of hands or at least to few, but as a rough generalization the common people (free peasants, traders and craftsmen) were a political force to be reckoned with from the sixth century onwards. This trend reached its brilliant climax in Athens.[3]

Even in Athens, it is true, political power never came into the hands of more than a minority. When Plato was a small boy, perhaps one man in six or seven out of the whole population was a citizen. The immediate 'reasons' are plain: one was the existence of slavery, marking the ultimate origin of these States in military conquest. In a sense, however, it was even more to do with the concept of who *should* enjoy political power, or citizenship, which in turn depended on the Athenians' self-perception. They perceived themselves as a kinship group; accordingly, citizenship *should* rest not on residence but on descent, on the father's side in one period, on both sides in

[1] Victor Ehrenberg, *The Greek State*, Blackwell, 1960, p. 11.

[2] ibid., p. 33.

[3] ibid., p. 23; M. I. Finley, *The Ancient Greeks*, Chatto and Windus, 1963, p. 50.

another. Persons of 'mixed' origin, freed slaves and immigrants had to be content with the status of aliens, or free non-citizens, like Aristotle himself. They were prominent in industry, commerce and banking, and indeed, except for land-holding, they enjoyed full civil rights. But almost invariably they were kept for ever outside the pale of the constitution.

These were limitations. Yet if the distribution of political power among the Athenian population as a whole was markedly unequal, it was so extensive among citizens during the fifth and fourth centuries that to speak of government by the people was almost as near to being literally true as is conceivable and certainly as the practice has ever been. Originating in the decade before the fifth century opened, and reflecting sociologically the pressure of one social class upon another and ideologically the growing impact of the Pythagorean notion of the equality of parts or members (i.e. an arithmetic as opposed to a proportionate equality), this rule of the 'whole people' became fully rooted and fruitful somewhere about the middle of the fifth century. It had four sets of institutions corresponding to the discharge of four broad functions. For legislation, including in practice many detailed decisions (e.g. on foreign affairs and defence, and finance), there was an assembly of indefinite tenure or duration, comprising all adult male citizens, and meeting, thanks to a balmy climate, in the open air. It was, of course, a mass-meeting; in the late fifth century, perhaps as many as 5000 turned out in peace-time. For certain kinds of business (e.g. ostracism) a quorum was as many as 6000.

The assembly normally met forty times a year, with extra sessions if required. Routine administration was carried on by magistrates, or, as we would say, officials or functionaries, although they were military as well as civil. Altogether there were some 350 of them at one period (late fourth century). Working full-time for (usually) a year, a magistrate considered a question, reached a decision and, above all, issued the orders. Under our system we look to the Cabinet for the supervision and co-ordination of the administration. In fifth and fourth-century Athens, the supervision of the magistrates was the task of the Council of 500 which, meeting every day except on festivals, also prepared the agenda for the assembly and acted as a general steering committee for it. This—the preliminary sifting and consideration—was its principal function; it was the nearest that the Athenians went to 'executive initiative'. The courts of law were both less and more than we might expect from the term itself and from modern institutions. On the one hand, these were large popular courts in which citizens played the dual role of judge and jury. On the other hand, the courts had a political role as the reviewing authority for the conduct of officials when their term of office was over. Tenure was indefinite in that citizens were permanently eligible (from thirty onwards) for the panel from which any particular 'jury' was drawn. The courts met regularly except on festivals and when the assembly was sitting, which meant assembling on some 300 days a year.

In form at least, then, these institutions provided for the direct, active participation of all citizens. Subject to some possible disqualifications (arising, for example, from an unpaid debt to the Treasury), all citizens served in the assembly at twenty, and in the other institutions at thirty; the moderate property qualification for the routine administrative work had fallen into disuse by the fourth century and it may not have been implemented even in the century before. With few exceptions, selection for service was by lot, which for the Athenians was the true democratic method as opposed to voting, which they held to be aristocratic since it favoured the well-known or distinguished. The exceptions were important: the generals in the fifth century; some high financial officers in the fourth. Yet it is true that the lot was almost universally used: for most of the administrative jobs, for the Council of 500 (drawn from the 'wards' and parishes of Athens and Attica in proportion to size), and for the courts (from a panel of 6000, itself chosen annually by lot).

At the same time, elaborate arrangements were made to circulate political power. Magistrates (=officials), if chosen by lot, as most of them were, could serve for only one year. Service in the Council of 500 was also limited to one year, with a lifetime maximum of two years in all. The assembly was convened by the presiding tribe (out of the ten tribes deemed to make up Athens). The role of presiding tribe was taken up by lot and in rotation, each tribe serving for about one tenth of a year, i.e. so to speak, for a rather long month. From the current presiding tribe came the assembly presidents, who, drawn by lot, served for twenty-four hours and no more. In the fifth century, a not dissimilar arrangement governed the choice of president for the Council of 500; in the fourth, presidents came from the nine non-presiding tribes.[4]

In such ways as these the Athenians went about as far as was organizationally possible (on their scale of operations) to enable the people (=citizens) to rule. But the organizationally possible may not be financially possible for many people. So the Athenians gradually took the next logical step: payment for service. By the fourth century, the magistrates were being paid at varying rates; the Council of 500 was being paid; the assembly *quorum* was being paid (first come, first 'served' in this other sense); while the empanelled juries were receiving subsistence. Contrary to older views, those who undertook public service were not 'on to a good thing'. The evidence is that the majority of citizens, perhaps six out of ten, worked with their own hands as peasant farmers, craftsmen, shop-keepers, seamen or labourers. Contrary again to earlier views, Athenian democracy was not parasitic on slavery. Late in the fourth century at least, most of the slaves were owned by the 1200 richest, out of a probable 21,000, citizens. The well-off citizens (say, 3000) owned most of the remainder. Thus most ordinary citizens had few slaves: think of the peasant farmer with five acres and possibly five slaves. It may well be true that slavery helped some common citizens in the sense of enabling the 'boss' to get off for the day. But generally the common citizen worked with his own hands, needed to be paid, and what he was paid scarcely amounted to more than compensation for his loss of working time.[5]

Here we touch the question: how far did the ordinary citizen actually participate? This is part of a wider question: did these institutions really work? The actual social composition of the various institutions is one guide. It is a difficult subject, partly because the comments of contemporary writers—anti-democrats almost to a man—cannot be wholly relied upon,[6]

[4] A. H. M. Jones, *Athenian Democracy*, Blackwell, passim but esp. ch. V.

[5] ibid., pp. 10, 17, 76. Also C. C. Field, *Political Theory*, Methuen, 1956, pp. 276–8. Finley, p. 71, agrees that payment really amounted to compensation.

[6] Jones, pp. 41–2; M. I. Finley, p. 71.

and because the scene changes not only from one century to another but from one institution to another. As between the two centuries, it seems that in the fifth the poorer citizens were rather more prominent than in the fourth, even perhaps in the Council of 500 where the preliminary scrutiny, the exacting duties and the fact of being held accountable for one's stewardship at the end of the year always combined to favour the 'middle-class' and well-to-do. By the fourth century, the jurors too, were predominantly 'middle-class', as was normally true even of the assembly.[7] In crises and on other special occasions, however, the 'working-class' turned out in force in the assembly, and throughout the classical period, the routine administration, being less exacting, was in their hands. In general, despite limitations imposed by innate capacity and by education and training, participation was fairly widespread.

In discussing whether the institutions really 'worked', we also have to explore in outline the actual relationship between assembly and Council. Was the assembly, even when peopled, as on great occasions, by the 'working-class', merely a rubber-stamp for the Council, which was for the most part 'middle-class' in composition? If we can distinguish between decrees and the more fundamental laws, which were in fact clearly separable only in the fourth century,[8] we can say that when the issue was uncontroversial, the Council would draft a decree, at times leaving some minor points to be settled by the assembly. A major issue would be placed as an item on the agenda and decided by the assembly. Experienced political 'in-fighters' will be quick to remark upon the potential significance of the Council's control of the agenda. In practice, however, an individual citizen could get an item on the agenda by working through a Councillor. Lacking influential friends at court, he could even write to the Council, and if the item were put on the agenda, he could then speak to it in the assembly. It is true that the Council might refuse (e.g. if the issue were judged frivolous), but it seems that they would not have rejected a reasonable request from anyone of some political standing. As a last resort, ordinary citizens might join forces in the assembly to propose that the Council should bring some matter forward for

[7] Jones, pp. 109 and 35–7.
[8] Jones, pp. 52 and 47.

consideration, even when it had not been previously dealt with. On balance, the Council's control of the agenda apparently amounted to very little.

When, in the fourth century, decrees became clearly distinguishable from laws, these were reviewed annually, according to a procedure that was more restrictive (a minimum age of thirty, legislative commissions, and the like); the effect of that was to reduce participation. On the other hand again, over and above both laws and decrees, there stood the popular courts, acting as a kind of United States Supreme Court, or guardian of the constitution.

Thus, despite understandable doubts (e.g. the Oxford historian, Trevor-Roper's), Athenian institutions in practice as well as on paper, did provide (as the outstanding reconstructions of the Cambridge ancient historian, A. H. M. Jones, disclose) a high degree of participation in the decision-making process. After listening, certainly, to the informed advice of quasi-professional leaders, individual citizens did make broad policy.[9] To a substantial degree, they also executed policy and took many detailed decisions. It has been estimated that on any given day, one citizen in four was engaged on some form or other of public service.[10] Two generations ago, that great Greek scholar-teacher, Lowes Dickinson, wrote that to be a citizen in classical Greece entailed 'a direct and active co-operation in all the functions of civil and military life'. If another Cambridge scholar, Jones, now discloses qualifications to that claim, it remains true that 'direct personal service was the cardinal point'. The citizen's 'whole ideal of conduct was inextricably bound up with his intimate and personal participation in public affairs'.[11] In relation to Athenian democracy specifically, that other Cambridge authority on the city-state, M. I. Finley, confirms that 'direct participation' was the key to it.[12]

* * * * *

[9] Jones, pp. 121–2, 124, 132, 111; H. R. Trevor-Roper, *New Statesman*, 31st May 1958.

[10] Walter Agard, *What Democracy Meant to the Greeks*, University of North Carolina, 1942, p. 72.

[11] Lowes Dickinson, *The Greek View of Life*, Methuen Vintage Books, 1941, pp. 71 and 134.

[12] Finley, p. 68.

But, it may be asked, did Athenian institutions work in the other senses of the term? Did they provide effective government? Did they induce a wider view, a capacity to relate remote causes and far-off events to personal interests, enabling (as Mill put it) 'one whose daily occupations concentrate his interests in a small circle round himself' to 'feel for and with his fellow-citizens', and to become 'consciously a member of a great community'?[13] It is also worth asking, since it bears directly upon the theory of motivation here adopted, whether widespread participation was followed by a great release of energies and creative talents of various kinds.

Despite the criticisms of contemporary writers, whose social bias, almost without exception, is striking, and of some nineteenth-century historians, such as Macaulay, who thought that the Athenians tended to become a mob, there is now a well-established tradition extolling the Athenians' political achievements. Picking up Macaulay's own phrase, Edward Freeman, the Oxford historian, retorted that—

> 'this mob clothed with executive functions made one of the best governments which the world ever saw. It did not work impossibilities; it did not change earth into paradise nor men into angels. . . . But that Government cannot be called a bad one which is better than any other government of its own time. And surely that government must be called a good one which is a marked improvement upon every government which has gone before it. The Athenian Democracy is entitled to both these kinds of praise. Demos was guilty of some follies and some crimes; but he was guilty of fewer follies and fewer crimes, and he did more wise and noble deeds, than any other government of his own or any earlier age.'[14]

Modern authorities reach much the same conclusion. 'This sort of government', Walter Agard, the American philosopher, remarks, directed the City-State during the hundred years of its greatest development, controlling for more than half a century its political, economic and legal relations with some two hundred and fifty states within the Athenian Empire. 'This is no mean achievement for any society; and especially for the

[13] John Stuart Mill, *Representative Government*, Blackwell, 1946, p. 211.

[14] Edward A. Freeman, 'The Athenian Democracy', in *Historical Essays*, second series, Macmillan, 1873, essay IV.

first democracy which controlled an empire it is a political triumph'.[15] Jones judges that by ancient standards, Athens was a remarkably efficient state; administratively, she was superior to most cities of that time. 'Incomparably' the most efficient naval power of the day, she governed an empire and managed its finances 'with notable success'. The system worked unchanged for almost two centuries.[16]

But how far did the institutions prove effective not simply in the sense that policy was formulated and efficiently executed by the standards of the time, but also in the sense of inducing civic virtue? The vagueness of the question must not be made an excuse for evading it. Suppose we take Mill's criterion as a very crude guide to the phenomenon we are looking for: how far did the citizen learn to relate remote causes and far-off events to personal interests? How far did the citizen learn to 'feel for and with his fellow-citizens', and to become 'consciously a member of a great community?'

At first glance, the answer suggested by several discussions is that no such feeling or consciousness was engendered. On the contrary, several of the received accounts, by non-Marxists as well as Marxists, are redolent of class conflict, even of class-war (presumably a severer form of class conflict).[17] In Greece generally, class conflict does, of course, hit the eye, especially in the seventh and sixth centuries,[18] when the growth of trade and handicrafts and the introduction of coinage were superimposed upon the scarcity of land as sources of class tension and bitterness. It was indeed this very class conflict that in large measure brought about the period of government by tyrants (from about the mid-seventh century to nearly the end of the sixth). For a century or so before that, political power had been in the hands of a landed aristocracy.[19] Often supported by the new trading class and by ordinary workers, the tyrants, who were then unconstitutional rather than brutal rulers, greatly eased the stresses of class conflict.

In Athens itself this trend came to a head towards the middle

[15] Agard, p. 75.

[16] Jones, ibid., p. 99, and *The Listener*, 2 Feb. 1961, p. 219.

[17] Margaret O. Wason, *Class Struggles in Ancient Greece*, Gollancz, 1947; C. M. Bowra, *The Greek Experience*, Mentor Books, 1962 ed., p. 93.

[18] Finley, *The Listener*, 12 Feb. 1959, p. 252.

[19] Finley, *The Listener*, 26 Jan. 1961, p. 178.

of the sixth century, when Peisistratus, by a *coup*, took command of the situation. Under his benevolent dictatorship, Athens gained some respite from class struggle and prospered economically: in silver mining, the manufacture of pottery and above all in the export of her specialized agricultural products. The rule of the tyrants lasted as long as the prosperity lasted. When, half a century later, the prosperity and even the independence of mainland Greece were threatened by the rise of Persia, which closed some markets and dislocated trade generally, the reigning tyrant fell. For a moment it looked as if the suppressed class conflict was about to be again unleashed, but the introduction of the democratic constitution (by an aristocratic family with commercial interests) tipped the scales decisively towards the new men—essentially the urban traders, manufacturers, artisans and labourers. Thus was continued the trend away from the rule of the aristocrats that the tyrants had already fostered.

What happened to class conflict during the period when the democratic constitution was in force? Some impressive authority (e.g. the Oxford classicist, Maurice Bowra's) suggests a perpetuation of class conflict and even of class-war. But some of his evidence is really of class *feeling*,[20] and is derived from imaginative literature, whose value as firm historical evidence is here even more difficult than usual to assess. As for Bowra's 'bloodthirsty counterpart in action' to expressions of class feeling, he cites only two instances, one of which occurred in Athens. To my admittedly Greek-less eyes, the actual overt class conflict in fifth-century Athens was remarkably small. The 'right-wing' *coup* in Athens in 404 B.C., when so many democrats were liquidated, was one of two, in the strict sense, reactionary moves or usurpations in the whole democratic period of about a century and three quarters. It happened in wartime when the end was in sight, and with the aid of the enemy's occupying army. And it is important to recall that the restoration of democracy the following year was done in a most generous, law-abiding and magnanimous spirit. Despite the liquidations of the previous year, there were no reprisals. As Freeman said, democratic Athens did not slay.[21] Instead an

[20] ibid., p. 92.
[21] ibid., p. 131.

amnesty was offered—the first, according to the historian Acton, in history; an amnesty, as Xenophon (no friend of democracy) remarked, that was actually kept. The other 'right-wing' *coup* (in 411 B.C.) also occurred in wartime. Significantly, it was launched when the fleet was mobilized. Unlike the army, the fleet was manned by the urban poor, who were accordingly absent, with leave, from the assembly.[22] Both affairs were the work of 'right-wing' extremists, who enjoyed only a little brief authority; democracy was restored, not by the urban poor alone but by the mass of citizens, including the men of substance.[23]

Less extreme instances of class conflict may be judged from the distribution of political power, the tone of the appeals made by the political leaders and the actual policies pursued. In the distribution of power and influence, the rich came off quite well: for instance they held many important military, diplomatic and financial offices. Orators in the assembly were often well-to-do.[24] As to the tone of the appeals made by the political leaders, it seems that the actual speeches survive only from the end of the fifth century, but from then onwards at least, such appeals were usually couched in national rather than sectional terms. There was little attempt to play off the poor against the rich.[25] Many policies commanded wide support. If in some policies, class divisions could be plainly seen, these did not automatically follow class lines: the rich and well-born could be found on the side of popular democracy. No oligarchical party arose based on the protection of property. Nor, on the whole, did the poor soak the rich. Recent judgments confirm W. L. Newman's almost a century ago that 'the wonder is the rich suffered as little as they did'.[26] Unlike some contemporary democracies, Athens never proposed to redistribute the land (that extremely scarce good) or to cancel debts. Surely Finley is right to conclude that Athens was *comparatively* free from 'stasis', or factionalism. And Jones's test surely applies: the 'best proof that the democracy satisfied

[22] Finley, *The Listener*, 5 Oct. 1961, p. 504.
[23] Jones, *The Athenian Democracy*, p. 42.
[24] Jones, p. 55.
[25] Finley, *The Listener*, 19 Oct. 1961, p. 559.
[26] W. L. Newman, op. cit., p. 505; Finley, ibid., p. 554.

all classes is that it lasted almost unchanged for two centuries'.[27] Even Bowra, more inclined, following Thucydides and others, to stress conflict, agrees that 'a working balance' was maintained between order and anarchy.[28]

Received views about class conflict and even class-war, therefore, have to be put in perspective and even corrected, at least for Athens. The truth is that much consensus lay beneath the surface of things. Everyone agreed on fundamentals, e.g., the rule of law and on the community as the source and arbiter of that law.[29] 'The majority of Athenians were proud of their constitution and deeply attached to it.'[30] It does not seem, therefore, that the accounts of class conflict in Greece should rule out of court, for Athens, an affirmative answer to the inquiry: did the new institutions induce a sense of feeling for and with one's fellow-citizens, some conscious identification with a wider community?

All the same, some more positive evidence would be welcome. There are some indications.[31] When the Persians cast their shadow over Greece, some Athenian leaders wanted to try to come to terms with them. But the new institutions had engendered a pan-Hellenic feeling, and early in the fifth century, against the advice of their leaders, the Athenians dispatched a small force to help a revolt of the Greeks of Ionia against the Persians. It was the new democracy that, within the next twenty years, defeated the mighty Persian Empire both on land (Marathon) and at sea (Salamis). Since the navy was recruited from the common citizens of Athens, the victory at sea is particularly significant. 'A few thousand free citizens' had defeated the Persian conscripts. 'Salamis', as the young R. H. S. Crossman observed, 'was the glorious justification of the new Athenian democracy.'[32]

Even the attacks on other Greek States are germane. For,

[27] Jones, ibid., pp. 91–2 and 131; Finley, ibid.

[28] Bowra, pp. 94–5.

[29] Finley, *The Listener*, 12 Feb. 1959, p. 289.

[30] Jones, ibid., p. 42.

[31] It is tempting to quote Sir Denis Brogan's scout at Balliol, who pointed out to the young man up from Glasgow that in Greek 'idiot' meant a private person, one who took no interest in public affairs. But I presume that this meaning antedates the period to which I refer.

[32] R. H. S. Crossman, *Plato Today*, Allen and Unwin, 2nd revised ed., 1959, pp. 27–8.

rightly or wrongly, these were initiatives taken in the name of a democratic community against autocratic regimes. In general, the Athenians did display a 'fierce independence and loyalty to their own community' and way of life, a 'powerful feeling of community', a marked 'community solidarity'.[33]

It seems possible to conclude, then, that the new institutions did provide effective government and that the Athenian citizen did escape from the constricting 'small circle round himself' and identify strongly with the wider community. But how far was this the consequence of the new element of widespread participation? No one can answer the question with certainty, but it has been generally thought that 'the common life of the Athenian was the best of political educations', providing a foundation for effective government. As for 'fierce independence and loyalty' or 'solidarity', this is what social science would lead us to expect to follow from increased participation; and for Athens the one thing has been linked to the other as cause and consequence by classical scholars. Lowes Dickinson, for instance, judged that 'the identification of the individual citizen with the corporate life delivered him from the narrow circle of personal interests into a sphere of wider views and higher aims'.[34] *Wider views and higher aims:* i.e. a widening of the ambit of men's altruism, a widening of their area of loyalty.

Some further support for this view of *participation* as the true energizing force in the new Athenian institutions may be drawn from the motivational theory made use of throughout this essay. Participation, of course, can be proposed or defended on the grounds of *politics*, i.e., as 'the basic method for establishing areas of agreement or political consensus', in which *political* judgment is exercised to achieve not final solutions but 'tentative stabilities within a situation of conflict'.[35] But participation is also *the* instrument for gratifying men's higher needs; accordingly, its widespread introduction and practice in Athens ought to have been accompanied by a substantial cultural flowering. What actually happened, of course, was a

[33] Finley, *The Listener*, 26 Jan. 1961, p. 178 and 12 Oct. 1961, p. 554.

[34] ibid., p. 134.

[35] Sheldon S. Wolin, *Politics and Vision*, American ed. 1960, Allen and Unwin, 1961, pp. 62 and 65. For an eloquent British statement, see Bernard Crick, *In Defence of Politics*, Weidenfeld and Nicolson, 1962.

great cultural explosion, still the most astonishing in the history of the West. Many close observers see a causal or conditioning relationship between the one thing and the other. Freeman was clear that 'the pre-eminence of Athens in literature, philosophy and art, was simply the natural result of her pre-eminence in freedom and good government'. For Agard the new democratic institutions '*created*' [my italics] 'a culture of the first order'. It was the political institutions that led the Greek spirit to its supreme cultural achievements after Homer, Ehrenberg concludes. Bowra's judgment is particularly apposite: once the Athenians found themselves in control of their own destiny, their powers were released in many new directions—poetry, drama, architecture, sculpture. So close is the connection considered to be that Bowra can even speak of 'the new democratic architecture'.[36]

Perhaps the classical scholars and ancient historians claim too much. They show little awareness of the social-psychological insight that the nature of the Athenian *self* recruited into the political roles must have had much to do with the success of the institutions and with the cultural explosion. Freeman is an exception to this generalization: he thought, for instance, that the political intelligence of the average Greek was higher than that of the average English M.P. of his day.[37] In a different way, Finley, too, is an exception, observing that the Greeks brought to the very concept and word, *polis* (or city-state), the idea of *community*.[38] No idea so 'buried' in concept and language could have been merely a product of institutional patterns. Yet in a complex interplay the new political institutions embodying participation must be given their due. We have only to compare the Athens of the fifth and fourth centuries with most of the previous century when the tyrants were in command to gain some rough idea of the 'difference' that participation made.

Putting all the pieces together, I think it reasonable to conclude that different institutions do have different ethical propensities, and in particular that political institutions embodying genuine *participation* will tend to induce civic

[36] Freeman, p. 109; Agard, p. 75; Ehrenberg, p. 27; Bowra, pp. 86–7.
[37] ibid., p. 174.
[38] *The Ancient Greeks*, pp. 88 and 46–8.

virtue. The non-citizen Aristotle saw the general truth very clearly: the form of government is an expression of the kind of life that the State is designed to foster. It is time that we took the lesson to heart.

CHAPTER FOURTEEN

A SONG UNFINISHED

'The only end of writing is to enable the readers better to enjoy life or better to endure it.' If Dr. Johnson's own writing provides the enjoyment, I realize that this essay of mine, if useful at all, contributes only to the endurance. It is written in full awareness of the fragility of the international order within which even the least comfortable among us live our sheltered and not unrewarding lives. It is written in full awareness, too, of the many domestic obstacles to reform in a world where, as Dr. Johnson also said, 'much is to be done and little to be known,' and where (to cite a really learned doctor, Aristotle) so much is at the mercy of Nature and Fortune. The more one looks, in particular, at our industrial institutions, the more one reads into a remark made in one of Carson McCullers' stories:

> ' "*L'improvisation de la vie humaine*", he said. "There's nothing that makes you so aware of the improvisation of human existence as a song unfinished. Or an old address book".'[1]

Or our factory system, as improvised, in a not dissimilar sense, somewhere between 1750 and 1850, and still, in human terms, unfinished.

Yet it is *partly* because international dangers abound that we must reform—to reduce the friction and the conflict, to promote more fruitful lives and a more cohesive community. Persian Empires are all around us, while our own colonizing Greeks are too remote, too small, too diluted to affect the balance of forces. Although we cannot be isolationists, we cannot look to others, either, for the material resources and skill to deploy, the energy to expend or the political imagination to bring these together in productive combinations. In that sense we stand alone; or fall alone. If posterity at large ever acknowledges a debt to us for, in the end, holding off Hitler, it will never dream

[1] in *The Ballad of the Sad Café*, Cresset Press, 1958, p. 154.

of paying our descendants. As for social knowledge, if it is not commensurate with our social obligations, it is enough to make a start. Our immediate problem is to apply what we already know or are reasonably sure of.

We know and can explain what earlier generations dimly felt or vaguely experienced—that an institution (or social group) is essentially a normative structure. That *is* what it is. We also know that the norms leave their mark on the character of the persons whose lives are bounded by them in their several social positions. We know, too, that the mark can be a stain, i.e. that institutions vary in their ethical (or educative) significance and consequences. Some give 'reality to the capacities of the will and reason in man' (in T. H. Green's phrase); others treat man as mindless protoplasm, to be pricked and prodded this way or that. Some open chinks on a wider realm; others direct men's gaze firmly at the ground. Some induce concern for others; some inhibit or even discourage it.

If we do not want the mark to be a stain, we know that we have to take the trouble to design an appropriate institutional pattern. Even for us, most favoured island, things do not happen of their own accord. In particular, we know that if we want to widen the ambit of men's altruism or loyalty, then we have to arrange for them to participate in the decision-making that touches their lives. Only participation can gratify men's higher needs. Aristotle taught that man was born for citizenship (or participation in decision-making in the *polis*) because it alone enables him to develop his capacities to the full. As with political man, so with industrial man, since, after all, the reality is simply *man* operating in different settings. We also know that the gratification of men's higher needs releases them from the bondage of *self* and the immediate circle; if participation and therefore gratification is sustained, men begin to grope their way towards larger circles, more enduring wholes, i.e. towards civic virtue.

The defining characteristic of this *participation* is that it is direct not indirect. Even the indirect form should not be angrily or wearily dismissed; it may be useful for satisfying the higher needs of the few who can take part as well as for underwriting some of the lower needs of the vast majority who cannot.

But for the making of responsible men, we must have responsible autonomy—a realm of direct participation.

In applying the idea of direct participation, we must not forget that the scale of operations, whether industrial, as in the Durham coalfield, or political, as in Athens (that larger Derby-in-Derbyshire), has always been small. That does not affect the validity of the idea (origin and validity being distinct issues), but it does affect its applicability. Smallness is significant for at least two reasons. In terms of the city-state, citizens ought not, as Aristotle said, to be too many to be taken in at a view, and although that is in part the local manifestation of a key idea of his,[2] it makes good practical sense too. Size or scale also bears upon the ethical influence of institutions. Precisely because Athens was small, its moral life would not seem beyond the shaping influence of law and institutions. The underlying belief was that moral influence could not be expected to travel far from its source. Men could not be spiritual guides to each other without knowing each other, without belonging to and living in one and the same city.[3] The English historian Peter Laslett makes much the same point in his discussion of the *polis* as a 'face-to-face' society, 'ready-made' rather than artificially created (like the House of Commons) and bound together by certain understandings.[4]

We are encouraged, then, to look to small groups for the translation of ideas into practice. We already know that the problem to be solved arises in the factory; it is there, under full employment, that the behaviour to be influenced actually occurs (e.g. the deliberate behaviour that brings about earnings-drift); it is there that the character of the young recruit is fashioned and set. So we take as our building-blocks the small, or primary, groups as these emerge 'ready-made' in the industrial process. Charted by sociologists, these become the

[2] e.g., a 'period' in composition ought to have that magnitude which can be taken in at a view; the plot of a tragedy should conform to certain lengths; a beautiful animal should be neither too big nor too small.

[3] W. L. Newman, op. cit., pp. 73–4.

[4] in Peter Laslett (ed.), *Philosophy, Politics and Society*, Blackwell, 1956, pp. 162–3. I do not think, however, that 'face-to-face' is an apt term for the polis. It glosses over the requirement of a quorum of 6000 for some assembly matters; even 1000 constitutes a mass-meeting. Above all the composition of the assembly was constantly changing (M. I. Finley, *The Listener*, 5 Oct. 1961, p. 504).

rocks on which a system of representation (or indirect participation) is constructed, but, above all, each should be granted a measure of responsible autonomy. That is to say, subject to variations according to plant, industry and other circumstances, structures must be designed to accommodate the deconcentration of some managerial authority to the level of the primary work-group. Within a pre-determined range, men must be given their head to take their own decisions, and to introduce on their own initiative some variety into their work, previously 'enlarged' by agreement with management. The distribution of the product would still be a source of dispute, but it would be the more rationally discussed and settled, the more the present frustration of the workers and its behavioural consequences were reduced. Sustained over a considerable period of time, the new institutional pattern would tend to produce a worker with a different character, who, in *learning* to look outside himself and his immediate circle to those on the incoming shift, would thereby take the first few steps towards *learning* a concern for the community as a whole.

How could such reforms be set in motion? It is natural to look first to the nationalized industries. It was under the auspices of the National Coal Board that the experiment in responsible autonomy was undertaken: it is in the electricity supply industry that the most gallant attempts have been made to bring joint consultation to life. But, from the standpoint of satisfying workers' needs, the nationalized sector as a whole is now a waste land. In order to make the gratification of those needs the *primary* purpose of nationalization, we shall have to re-trace our steps to the fork in the road where the Labour Movement followed the Fabians instead of the Guild Socialists, who alone had some of the elements of a theory of motivation. In the words of the Belgian socialist and professor of social economics, Henri de Man, lecturing at the Labour College at Frankfurt in the 1920s, the broad principle of reconstruction must be this:

> 'The actual producers' joy in their work, and, consequently, in great measure their effective productivity, will not be so much promoted by any centralist reform of the relations of ownership, as by a local reform of working conditions in respect of working technique and in respect of hierarchical workshop organization.

> The essential thing is the formation of a new group consciousness within the individual enterprises. The touchstone of the effectiveness of any centralist change in property relations will, therefore, always primarily be the question, how far the change will tend to awaken this group consciousness on democratic lines, by arousing a keener sense of responsibility and by promoting the joys of self-determination.'[5]

In short, our aim must become 'socialization from beneath' socialization on the psychological basis of working solidarity and of a healthy democratic esprit de corps in the individual enterprise', not 'socialization from above', although this 'is the easier, because the paper on which laws and ordinances are written is more patient than are human beings'.[6] Two generations the wiser, we can testify to the truth of that vision. Fortunately, it is not too late to try again. We can begin by taking what we now have—nationalization from above—and turning it into 'socialization from beneath' through the instrument of 'free but responsible' groups. For this purpose the Government and Parliament would have to re-define not only the goal of nationalization but also their own relationship to the publicly-owned industries, which is in any case desirable. Secondly, in any future proposals to nationalize, I should make my first and crucial test, even before taking a bearing on Aneurin Bevan's 'commanding heights of the economy': does it or does it not seriously try to satisfy the higher needs of the workers, i.e. genuinely provide for direct participation, or responsible autonomy?

Without a telescope to my eye, I do not, in any case, see so many commanding heights waiting to be scaled, although I do see with the naked eye some dirty wells to be cleaned out and a few sunny, upland pastures that might as well be occupied. Empirically, too, it is perfectly obvious that, for better or worse, we have as a community about reached a point of balance as between the private and public sectors. A little more; a little less—that, short of some convulsion, is about the size of it for the coming generation. It follows that for extensions of responsible autonomy, we must look to private industry. The obstacles are not as great as they might at first appear:

[5] Henri de Man, *Joy in Work*, Allen and Unwin, 1929, p. 53.
[6] ibid., p. 54.

we really must not allow ourselves to be bewitched by words and forms. 'Socialization from beneath' is as conceivable in private industry as in public. Under the regime of Lord Brown of Machrihanish and Elliott Jaques at the Glacier Metal Company, it would not have taken much to tip the scales towards responsible autonomy in the sense defined.[7] So, too, with those plants in the United States and Britain (e.g. Pressed Steel, Scotland) in which the Scanlon Plan or one of its variants has been in operation; or where the ideas of Douglas McGregor, who taught Industrial Management at M.I.T., have been fruitful. What matters is not ownership as such but the reality of sharing decisions in industry, and all that that implies for the gratification of men's root-needs, for the shaping of a certain type of character, and so for the quality of British life. In the 1920s, Henri de Man pleaded that socialism should assert its moral character; today, socialization must make that same affirmation, and when argued for, produce the same credentials. And in that sense, a socialized private factory is as conceivable as one in public ownership.

As conceivable, but not, I agree, as likely. Even more than a nationalized industry, private industry defines its objectives in terms other than the gratifying of its own workers' needs: its objectives can be variously stated as survival, making a profit, meeting consumer demand. The workers' needs come into the reckoning only marginally as those biogenic needs that have to be manipulated instrumentally in the cause of production, i.e. as one element in a distorted theory of motivation. Joined to this obstacle is the fear of what would happen were managerial authority to be deconcentrated, i.e., surrendered. In the end, the problem is one of sheer ignorance. Private managers must be taught to recognize the economic costs incurred in our present organization: the costs of frustration, as revealed, directly or indirectly, in restrictive practices, voluntary absenteeism, avoidable accidents, day-dreaming and strikes; as also the cost of value foregone—of what would be produced if industry elicited the willing, self-disciplining co-operation of

[7] Wilfred (now Lord) Brown, *Exploration in Management*, Heinemann, 1960; Elliott Jaques, *The Changing Culture of a Factory*, Tavistock Publications with Routledge and Kegan Paul, 1951.

its workers,[8] and if managers themselves were thereby freed to play a really creative role. Private managers must also be taught to recognize the political costs incurred in our present social organization: that they produce men as well as goods, and that these men constitute the raw material of politics.

Who is to be responsible for dispelling this ignorance? Some enlightenment may come from the new business schools and related sources, but the main responsibility should be the Government's. This is not only because the immediate problems (inflation, balance of payments) are national or because the dispelling of ignorance would in practice have to be accompanied by inducements to change derived from the public purse, for example, from tax concessions, or from the Government's acquiring a large or controlling share in this or that firm. It is also because we ought in any case to revive the Greek notion that the business of politics (as of political science) does include the shaping of citizens through institutions, the designing of forms of government (or decision-making) that contribute to the good life. Since the coming of the factory system, 'institutions' must be industrial no less than political in the conventional sense. Thus, in private as well as in nationalized industry, we must look to a Government initiative, an initiative based on no other dogma than that industry should at least try to satisfy the workers' root-needs as fully as possible, an initiative based on no grand design but on a study of evolutionary trends and on a determination 'to open accessible trails'.[9]

It is not only management, however, that the Government (any Government) will have to teach; it is also, of course, the unions. What is wanted is a trade union organization to match the reconstructed industrial organization. But here the longest way round is the shortest way home. If the argument throughout has been more or less on the right lines, neither this nor any other major trade union reform can be induced by exhortation, i.e. by talk. If the unions are to be changed, unionists have to change, and unionists have to be caught young as workers. The right sort of teaching would be the right sort of factory structure, in which the workers' higher needs were more fully

[8] See above Part II; also Rensis Likert, "Measuring Organizational Performance", *Harvard Business Review*, vol. 36, no. 2, March–April, 1958, p. 48.

[9] Henri de Man, p. 143.

satisfied and out of which, ultimately, a new type of man would tend to come.

It is at this point that one hears the siren voices. Since the root of the trouble is in industry, why not gradually contract out of the situation through increased automation and hence increased leisure? It is a very old dream, in direct descent from Antipater, not the Macedonian general who destroyed Athenian democracy but the Greek poet of Cicero's day. Thinking of the relief that the invention of the water-wheel for grinding corn would bring to female slaves, he wrote:

> 'Cease from grinding, ye women who toil at the mill; sleep late, even if the crowing cocks announce the dawn. For Demeter [goddess of the corn] has ordered the nymphs to perform the work of your hands, and they, leaping down on top of the wheel, turn its axle, which, with its revolving spokes, turns the heavy concave Nisyrian millstones. We taste again the joys of the primitive life, learning to feast on the product of Demeter without labour.'[10]

'Sleep late, even if the crowing cocks announce the dawn': it has a certain pastoral charm—but the idyllic life is not for us. It is already plain that leisure cannot satisfy men, not even leisure with abundance. This is not simply because some of men's root-needs (e.g. for affection or achievement) cannot curl up and patiently attend the close of even a very short working day. It is also because what happens at work profoundly shapes our capacity to enjoy, even to make anything of, our leisure. This is perhaps in part what the English economist, Joan Robinson means by saying that 'Full Employment' has become a right-wing slogan, tending to make employment an end in itself and masking the question of its content—what work is *for*.[11] At all events, after years of doing a job, it becomes us, *is* us. Each of us is one man, not two men; our lives form a continuum. If, adapting a remark by the American sociologist, David Riesman, the worker does not live humanely on the job, then leisured man will be unable to live humanely off it.

There is no escape, then, from grappling with the problem where it actually arises. But institutions, too, form a continuum.

[10] ibid.

[11] *Economic Philosophy*, Watts, 1962, p. 95.

The responsible autonomy that we seek to inject into our industrial order must also be injected into our political order, supplementing participation of the traditional kind, such as in voting. We can start by reversing the current constitutional theory governing the activities of local authorities, which is that they can do only that which has been specifically authorized by Parliament or Ministry. Instead they could be allowed to do anything that has not been specifically forbidden, and so become free to use their initiative. Between the local and the central a new system of elected regional authorities should be interposed, operating upon a sort of 'collective contract'. Regional authorities, that is to say, would receive from the central government a substantial range of powers in planning, land use and housing; in economic development and transport; in education, health and welfare as well as in the police and fire services.[12]

Thus we construct a series of circles or levels, possibly interlocking, each of which enjoys a measure of responsible autonomy. But that would be only a beginning; we must not lose sight of the ultimate aim—the shaping of a certain type of person or character. It follows that we should try to widen the sources of recruitment. Some local councils are largely composed of ineffectual gentlemen, bucolic farmers, twittering shopkeepers and superannuated trade-union officials, whose common denominator is that they have time to spare, that their attendance entails no financial loss and that they give the appearance of having been broken at the wheel. We must not only pay more generously for public service; it must be so arranged that to stand for any public office becomes a statutory right, guaranteed by the Government and enforced by the Courts. It must be a meaningful right, with annual increments, and so far as possible, promotion, accumulating 'for credit'.

By such measures we can undoubtedly improve what the Italian political scientist, Gaetano Mosca, called 'recruitment from below'. Yet the limitations are obvious too; the number who can actually *learn* by *doing* remains smaller than the public good requires. So we must try to engage the attention of a wider public through the adult education system and through tele-

[12] Cf. the proposals of Liberal Party candidates in the North-West, *The Guardian*, 12 July 1965.

vision and radio, and to stimulate informed discussion throughout the land. Mill's statement will stand repetition and universalizing:

> 'It is by political discussion that the manual labourer, whose employment is a routine, and whose way of life brings him in contact with no variety of impressions, circumstances, or ideas, is taught that remote causes, and events which take place far off, have a most sensible effect even on his personal interests; and it is from political discussion, and collective political action, that one whose daily occupations concentrate his interests in a small circle round himself, learns to feel for and with his fellow-citizens, and becomes consciously a member of a great community.'[13]

Responsible autonomy, then, in plants, mines and the larger offices wherever the technology provides 'organizational choice'; a local government system permitting councillors to undertake, within the general law, anything that has not been specifically forbidden; regional authorities with important powers and some financial independence; with, at all political levels, statutory rights and facilities to improve recruitment from below—all within the matrix of informed, nation-wide debate. But how shall we make it 'informed'? Obviously, the corollary of what has been so far suggested is reform of our educational system. In part it would amount to a radical improvement in the quality of the existing State provision for the purpose of improving the capacity to participate in some sense at some level. This would mean a school system less dedicated to the collection and transmission of 'facts' and much more to training not only the intelligence but also the qualities of initiative, originality and imagination. But in part it would require a marked change of emphasis to permit the education of the moral sympathies. We should begin to make conscious what is now only unconscious or half-hearted: the inculcation of values, not excluding new values or the re-interpretation of old ones.

It is not only changes in content, however, that we require but changes of structure. Aristotle again made the essential point all those centuries ago. Long before the Jesuits, he saw and taught the meaning of the education of the young for the formation and improvement of national character, which was

[13] *Representative Government*, Blackwell, 1946, p. 211.

itself the beginning of constitutional improvement. But the prerequisite for success, he taught, is that education ought to be one and the same. This meant two things: both the control of education (which in Athens was in private hands) and the pursuit of it should be public, i.e. education should be by the State and in common. We have fulfilled the first condition but not the second. On the contrary, by one of those mischievous tricks played on us by a grinning Fate, as education in general became public in the nineteenth century, there took place the greatest wholesale extension of the private sector that our country has experienced. This is not only false to our history: in the age of the first Queen Elizabeth the grammar schools had boys representing a cross-section of the community. It is also silly if we wish to give boys and girls a sense of being part of an enduring whole, whose claim on one's loyalty is to take precedence (as in wage restraint or some other vital element in an urgent national policy) over loyalty to one's immediate circle or social group. Aristotle is surely right: those who are to work together as members of the same State should be educated in the same way and educated together, with a firm 'public' stamp upon the education itself. Thus the State and the private sectors should be merged.

Concurrently (and any worthwhile reforms have to be concurrent), we require a first-class system of adult education. We have to continue the education, in the usual sense, of the young men entering the factory, so that they develop their capacities to make use of responsible autonomy when they get it. By the same token we require it to enable citizens to participate in the political realm. Running through it all should be a concern for values, traditional and emergent—a continuation of that education of the moral sympathies which should have started in the schools. It would include the re-education of parents.

Obviously, such reforms as these would demand great effort and much sacrifice. But the prize is correspondingly great. For the industrial roles are, so to speak, extrapolated on to the larger screen of the community to form the outline of our social class system; the frustrations experienced in the factory and the concomitant behaviour make for what Mill in 1848 called 'the widening and embittering feud between the class of labourers and the class of capitalists', which, reflected and reinforced by the educational system, becomes 'the split society'.[14] Mill could put it that way only because the capitalists were then the managers; the standing feud is really between worker and manager. Nor was Mill's own remedy—'some sort of co-operative system'—at all adequate; he seems to have meant little more than profit-sharing. But he had the historical sense to formulate the problem—

> 'The problem is, to obtain the efficiency of production on a large scale, without dividing the producers into two parties with hostile interests, employers and employed, the many who do the work being mere servants under the command of the one who supplies the funds, and having no interest of their own in the enterprise, except to fulfil their contract and earn their wages.'[15]

It dogs us still; indeed it is now far more acute. For, thanks to full employment, it is more than ever true that, as he put it in his own day—

> 'The poor have come out of leading-strings, and cannot any longer be governed or treated like children. To their own qualities must now be commended the care of their own destiny.'[16]

Hence, the well-being of a people must be secured by means of the justice and self-government of the individual citizens. Now, 'The theory of dependence attempts to dispense with the necessity of these qualities in the dependent classes'. But it is the virtues of independence that they stand in need of, and such the Governments and the higher classes can promote, but only by treating the labouring classes as equals and openly. 'The prospect of the future depends on the degree in which they [the labouring classes] can be made rational beings'.[17]

Subject to re-interpretation, that is still true. In begging the unions to keep actual earnings within the annual increase in productivity, the Government is asking them to behave as rational beings. Are we ready to pay Mill's price? The current price would be substantial. In industry and commerce—the

[14] Nicholas Davenport, *The Split Society*, Gollancz, 1964.

[15] *Principles of Political Economy*, John W. Parker, 1848, vol. II, Book IV, pp. 323 4.

[16] ibid., pp. 318–19.

[17] ibid.

surrender of some managerial authority; for unions and union leaders—the loss of identity in some sort of industrial unionism; in politics, the opening up of the decision-making process. For the middle-class taxpayer, a substantial levy to train and pay a whole new breed of schoolteachers and other educationists. For the upper-middle class (and, even more seriously, the middle-class social climbers into the upper-middle class), the surrender of the right to *buy* an exclusive private school education for their children (and *through* that, probably, to gain entrance for them into Oxford and Cambridge), i.e. the right to divide children into two sections and the community into two realms. For Churchmen, the price would be the effort to re-interpret Christianity in terms of an industrial civilization (as in the lives of the worker-priests).

Of course, these reforms could not in general be imposed. On the private schools issue, for instance, nothing could be achieved unless middle-class parents were prepared to give way for the public good, since those schools reflect the power of money, which can be limited and civilized but not destroyed. So, too, with the other issues. A Government could lead but not impose; the interests, for the most part middle-class, would have to make genuine sacrifices for the long-term good of Britain. Are they—are *we*—prepared to make these? I do not know the answer, but since no one can say what the answer would be if the Government touched off and fostered the debate and the research, I do not despair of it either. One thing at least is certain. Once probed, the issue is not simply the civic obligation of the worker or of the unions; it is the civic obligation of us all.

INDEX OF NAMES

INDEX OF SUBJECTS